THE INNER GAME OF ENTREPRENEURING

10 Steps to Mastering the Small Business Challenge

Ronald E. Guzik

Upstart Publishing Company®
Specializing in Small Business Publishing
a division of Dearborn Publishing Group, Inc.

This publication is designed to provide accurate and authoritative information in regard to the subject matter covered. It is sold with the understanding that the publisher is not engaged in rendering legal, accounting, or other professional service. If legal advice or other expert assistance is required, the services of a competent professional person should be sought.

Acquisitions Editor: Jean Iversen
Managing Editor: Jack Kiburz
Editorial Coordination: John Patrick Grace, Grace Associates, Ltd., at Publishers Place, 945 4th Ave., Suite 200A, Huntington, WV 25701, 304-697-3236
Interior Design: Lucy Jenkins
Cover Design: DePinto Studios
Typesetting: the dotted i

© 1999 by Ronald E. Guzik

Published by Upstart Publishing Company®,
a division of Dearborn Publishing Group, Inc.

All rights reserved. The text of this publication, or any part thereof, may not be reproduced in any manner whatsoever without written permission from the publisher.

Printed in the United States of America

99 00 01   10 9 8 7 6 5 4 3 2 1

Library of Congress Cataloging-in-Publication Data
Guzik, Ronald E.
    The inner game of entrepreneuring : 10 steps to mastering the small business challenge / Ronald E. Guzik.
        p.   cm.
    Includes index.
    ISBN 1-57410-119-6 (pbk.)
    1. Small business—Management.   2. Entrepreneurship.   I. Title.
HD62.7.G89   1998
658.02′2—dc21   98-36904
                                                                              CIP

Upstart books are available at special quantity discounts to use as premiums and sales promotions, or for use in corporate training programs. For more information, please call the Special Sales Manager at 800-621-9621, ext. 4514, or write to Dearborn Financial Publishing, Inc., 155 North Wacker Drive, Chicago, IL 60606-1719.

PRAISE FOR *THE INNER GAME OF ENTREPRENEURING* . . .

"The success or failure of running a business probably has more to do with the physical and mental feelings of the person involved than with almost any other activity in life. And yet, few entrepreneurs really have a plan to remain as 'visionary' as they were when they started. Ron Guzik's new book, *The Inner Game of Entrepreneuring,* provides a step-by-step process to guide entrepreneurial owners to continually return to the inner sense of accomplishment and satisfaction that motivated them to go out on their own."

—Jeff Williams, President, Creative Market Solutions, Inc., Entrepreneurial Trainers

"*The Inner Game of Entrepreneuring* offers a valuable and unusual way to understand the personal issues involved in starting and managing a new venture. Guzik skillfully balances insights into the entrepreneurial process with simple exercises to put those insights to work. I particularly like his ideas on understanding the importance of feelings on business. This alone would have saved me a lot of time and grief if I had read it during my entrepreneurial days! I enthusiastically recommend this book to any entrepreneur—indeed, anyone who has to manage others."

—David H. "Andy" Bangs, Jr., Author, *The Business Planning Guide*

"I only wish I could have read *The Inner Game of Entrepreneuring* 13 years ago when I started my business . . . it certainly would have given me a leg up. As a Life Coach who works with entrepreneurs, I'll certainly recommend it to start-ups as well as seasoned business professionals. Thanks, Ron, for sharing your great insights!"

—Mershon Shrigley, Life Coach, Shrigley & Associates, Schaumburg, Illinois (www.womansadvanage.com/bwa)

"Ron Guzik has focused precisely on the basic and significant aspects of the creative and complex role of entrepreneurial leadership: the use of your own personality as the primary instrument for moving the business forward."

—James N. Farr, Author, *Supra-Conscious Leadership: New Thinking for a New World*

DEDICATION

To my family—my parents, Bev and Jim, and my brother and sisters, Jim, Linda, and Patti—who have supported me in everything I've done.

Contents

Foreword **ix**
Acknowledgments **xi**
Introduction **xiii**

STEP 1
Be Aware of Yourself as Well as Your Business **1**

STEP 2
Harness the Positive Power of Attention **15**

STEP 3
Recognize Mind-Sets That Help or Hurt Your Company **33**

STEP 4
Understand the Influence of Feelings on Business **54**

STEP 5
Light Your Entrepreneurial Fire **79**

STEP 6
Build Strong Business Habits **93**

STEP 7
Increase Your Personal Productivity **111**

STEP 8
Evaluate Your Business Systems **135**

STEP 9
Energize Your Work Environment **155**

STEP 10
Achieve Productive Synergy in Your Business **169**

Epilogue—Practice, Practice, Practice! **189**
Suggested Reading **191**
Index **197**

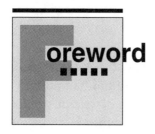

Foreword

A highly marketable skill or product does not guarantee success in business. Neither do adequate capitalization, good accounting, hard work, and sacrifice. What ordinarily passes for good management may not be sufficient either—not when profit margins are thin and time is short.

Something else is needed, and Ron Guzik has discovered what it is: in-depth knowledge of one's own personality, skills base, mind-sets, habits, and desires. With such knowledge of oneself, it becomes infinitely easier to read other people and figure out how to turn them into clients or customers.

I first met Ron four years ago when my husband and I were starting *Svoboda's Business Magazine.* Because of corporate downsizing, many talented people were opening their own businesses; there was an explosion of entrepreneurship.

Entrepreneurs ourselves, we positioned our magazine as an information source that would help bolster fledgling businesses. We were looking for experts on business topics who had important things to say. We quickly discovered that Ron Guzik was a man with a mission. He overflowed with new ideas to help individuals manage themselves and their employees more productively. Already a well-regarded teacher in several area adult-education programs, Ron wanted to reach a larger audience. He came to us with some ideas for articles. We listened.

Ron showed us how a lack of self-knowledge could be as fatal to an entrepreneur as any gap in business education or knack for sales or marketing. Without adequate self-knowledge, we fall victim to our own unrecognized bad habits and well-camouflaged fears. These demons can drag down our profits and stymie our growth. We were happy to launch Ron as an incisive commentator on all things personal and corporate having to do with entrepreneurial success.

Over the past few years, we've watched as Ron made his telling points on our pages. He has never for a moment downplayed the importance of such traditional business elements as supply and demand, marketing techniques, and various approaches to accounting. Nonetheless, Ron has demonstrated that such factors as "self-talk" (your inner dialogue), habits that go back to your childhood, and your attitudes toward other people are critical to whether you will succeed or fail in business.

In *The Inner Game of Entrepreneuring*, with absolute respect for your time and individuality, Ron will take you through principles, examples, and exercises that will help you identify what you personally need to change in yourself and how to chart a path to accomplish those changes. To work hand in hand with Ron is to lay the foundation for building an enterprise that will maintain a human focus *and* generate more profits than you may have dreamed possible.

—Jill Cleary-Svoboda
Editor, *Svoboda's Business Magazine*

Acknowledgments

Writing a book is often the work of many minds. I wish to express my appreciation and gratitude for the support of the following people:

- First and foremost is John Patrick Grace, my editorial consultant. Without Patrick this book literally would not have been published. Patrick was one of the first people who saw the vision and value of my work. Besides acting as a skillful writer and editorial consultant, Patrick also was my coach, agent, adviser, and friend.
- Next I want to thank Danielle Egan-Miller, former acquisitions editor at Dearborn Financial Publishing. Danielle saw the vision of the book and led us through the initial publishing process.
- The staff at Dearborn all were very wonderful and helpful, including Cynthia Zigmund, Bobbye Middendorf, Christine Litavsky, Jean Iversen, Jack Kiburz, Trey Thoelcke, and especially Sandy Holzbach, senior editorial assistant.
- Jill Cleary-Svoboda and Al Svoboda of *Svoboda's Business Magazine* have helped my career enormously. Besides launching my written work, they have encouraged and supported me since 1994. I enjoy knowing them and am honored to write for their magazine. I want particularly to thank Jill who took time out of her busy schedule to write a wonderful foreword.

- I am proud and thankful to teach or to have taught at the following schools: William Rainey Harper College, Oakton Community College, and the adult education programs at High School District 211 and High School District 200.
- I also am thankful to the many business owners and would-be business owners who have trusted my advice as a consultant.
- The authors of the books and tapes in the recommended reading list have contributed to my work enormously. I wish to thank and acknowledge them and say, "Buy their books and tapes!"
- The following people have contributed to my life and influenced my work: Rich Devos, Werner Erhard, Lou Tice, Anthony Robbins, Jack Canfield, Mark Victor Hansen, Mike and Sara Matoin, and Marshall Rosenberg.
- Finally, and most importantly to me, I wish to thank and express my appreciation for my friends who have loved and supported me in this project and in life: Chris Duros, Nancy and Richard Hartmann, Laura Vaughn, Peg Miller, Laura Beard, Susan Francis, Jamie Henderson and Leslie Harris, Kathy Hirsch, Zanne Gray, Lynn Pigott, Jim Gruber, Bruce Anderson, Roger Coon, Jeff Johnson, Lon Withers, Ronnie Stowell, Marilyn Pearson, Kathy Corra, Cameron Chase, A. J. Spence, Margarite Mathis, Mary Elizabeth Murphy, Sandy Karn, Tim and Karen Sheehan, Susan Heitsch, Linda Soto, Mershon Shrigley, and Jacqueline Miller.

Introduction

Welcome to the inner game of entrepreneuring. It's a game you are already playing, whether you realize it or not. You're much better off if you *do* realize it—if you can size up the dimensions of the playing field and get an understanding of the rules and the skills involved.

Would you play tennis or chess with professionals when you yourself are physically or mentally out of shape, or haven't even mastered the basic moves and strategies? You may be doing just that in your day-to-day running of your business. As you move along you'll see that the toughest opponent on the court is likely not the competition or the economy, but your own less-than-aware self. Never mind trying to conquer the competition. Until you can know and work with your own counterproductive mental models, habits, and practices, you're only beating yourself.

Developing a business is like putting up a building. Your business needs a foundation; a door so that you can invite the world in; windows to bring in some fresh air; and a good, solid roof to protect you from the elements. And there you are, scurrying around on the emerging structure, carrying an assortment of tools on your belt and using different tools where you think they will do the job. Tools such as planning, budgeting, inventory control, or advertising can—and may already—serve you well. There are additional tools, however, that can help you mightily in your efforts to build a solid structure—tools that you may well be missing or using poorly.

These tools have names, and you will get to know the meanings behind the names quite intimately as you trek through the terrain of *The Inner Game of Entrepreneuring*. I'm referring to:

- Awareness
- Attention (sharp focusing)
- Mind-sets or mental models
- Feelings
- Desires
- Habits
- Time management
- Systems thinking
- Environment
- Synergy

Perhaps you've been using some of these tools all along and have been calling them by other names. For instance, "awareness" may relate directly to what you have been calling "business experience." "Mind-sets" may sometimes be called "drives" or "inclinations." Habits are just habits, except that many of us are only superficially aware of how our own habits operate and either advance or block our progress.

The good news is that you will not have to plough through encyclopedias or training manuals searching for the tools I've listed above. You will not have to take seminars, go on a search through an online catalog, or interview successful businesspeople. I'm offering all of the tools you'll need in one handy book.

Some of these tools go way back in the history of human thought and skills building. A number are ancient and time-tested techniques, referred to by classical thinkers. Others have a modern twist. For instance, Howard Gardner, an eminent education professor at Harvard University, developed a theory of multiple intelligences. Two of these intelligences are the intrapersonal (self → self) and interpersonal (self → others) skills taught in this book. I will tailor the understanding of these skills to the needs of today's entrepreneurs, with examples that will appeal to the solo consultant, restauranteur, inventor, or spearhead of a manufacturing process, as just a few examples.

The first part of the inner game will show you a range of *intrapersonal* skills. These skills help you to understand yourself better—and the impact you have on people with whom you work and on the processes you oversee. The second part of the inner game will focus on *interpersonal* skills, on applying this material to external aspects of behavior (e.g., habits, time management) and to business conditions such as systems and work space environment. And I'll make the connection for you between these two kinds of skills.

To an astonishing degree, I have found the person who radiates success will be someone who is aware, attentive, and savvy about his or her own personality, patterns of thought, speech, and action—and their *impact on other people.* Such a person is then well equipped—as a consequence of developing keen self-awareness—to be aware of what makes *other people* tick. If you know what makes other people tick, you will know (1) how to sell yourself and your products effectively and build a solid customer or client base, (2) how to hire and develop a good team, and (3) how to create productive relationships with suppliers and others who inhabit the world of your business life.

This book is designed as a process where each step builds on the step before. Don't try to rush your reading, jump ahead, or skip around. Savor each step as it comes, and you will receive the maximum value from the material. If you embrace the process, coaxing aside your inclinations to resist whatever may initially seem foreign or threatening to your ego, this material can effect transformational changes in the way you see yourself, others, and situations that impact on your venture.

Some of the transformational power comes from heightened capacity to make finer and finer distinctions. Serious students of music can distinguish many things in the music they hear, tones and nuances the casual listener would not hear. Such an ability to distinguish keys, harmonies, dissonance, the contributions of individual instruments, and so forth, equips professionals to critique a symphony—or play a role in presenting one or even in composing one. The same holds true for the task of creating your business. Power to make distinctions between people, markets, products, and processes translates into power to make good decisions, which in turn translates into greatly increased chances of being successful.

I recommend that you try on the methods and techniques I'll be explaining as you would try on a new coat. Wear them for a little while. Walk around in them. See how they fit. You don't need to buy into every single technique I mention to profit from the book. But don't make the mistake of throwing away a whole closetful of ideas or new skills just because one doesn't fit you perfectly.

Only repeated use, sometimes for weeks or even months, will allow you to determine whether a skill or an approach will make a positive difference for you. Some of these methods will require persistence on your part to adapt them to your personality and your entrepreneurial environment. Be patient. You may not see immediate benefits. Down the road a little ways, after you have made some of these techniques your own and they have become second nature, the benefits should be substantial.

One final hint: Working on this book with a partner will magnify its impact on both of you. Learning to play the inner game well is a major challenge. Learning with a partner will increase your pleasure as well as your capacity to digest the material—and will heighten your chances for true and productive change.

I will help you chart your progress. At the end of each step is a quiz that measures your entrepreneurial quotient (or E.Q.) for that skill. Each quiz will tell you how well you perform the different steps of the inner game. Because each step is built on previous ones, if you don't do well on a quiz, revisit and reabsorb that step. The total for each step tells you how well you're doing on that skill; the grand total at the end of Step 10 tells you how well you're mastering the total inner game of entrepreneuring.

Good wishes and Godspeed on your journey.

—Ronald E. Guzik

Be Aware of Yourself as Well as Your Business

Confine yourself to the present.
—Marcus Aurelius

Awareness is *always* the beginning of change, and therefore the first step in measuring your entrepreneurial quotient—or E.Q. The small business owner who perceives what is happening in the present, who sees things in all their multiple aspects—both internal and external—has a tremendous advantage over a competitor who is less aware.

If the marketplace is in flux, you should be aware of impending change. Being unaware of market conditions can hurt and sometimes kill off a venture.

Are your employees satisfied with their working conditions and atmosphere, or not? Not recognizing your employees' unhappiness will probably deepen their displeasure with you. Being aware of why they are *happy* working for you will help you make good personnel decisions in the future.

Being aware of such unpleasant realities as tax obligations, new competitive pressures in the marketplace, or looming increases in rent, utilities, or other fixed monthly expenses will help you make good decisions. And, in building a team that is in synch with you in taking your venture to the top, a capacity for in-depth awareness is a critical skill.

Perhaps this is why the Harvard Business School newsletter called awareness the number one management skill of the next ten years.

Unawareness usually consists of not knowing that you don't know. This kind of not knowing—popularly termed *denial*—is sharply different from simply knowing that you do not know something. Most of us don't know quantum physics, and we realize that we don't know it. If we want to learn quantum physics, we understand that we will have to put time and energy into studying it. But not knowing that we don't know, *that* can be dangerous. As Louis Armstrong once said, "Some people, if they don't know, you can't tell them."

When visiting a large metropolitan area with which we are unfamiliar, we need to adopt the street smarts to move about in crowds safely. Otherwise, we are liable to be pickpocketed, have a purse or briefcase snatched, or perhaps find ourselves in danger of being physically harmed. To refuse to adjust our consciousness from the way we think and behave in the comfort of our own town is to invite trouble.

In developing a new venture—perhaps having come from the relatively safe environment of a college campus or employment in the public sector—we can quickly find ourselves in trouble if we ignore the many risks that may arise. Such risks may stem from exploitive commercial landlords, litigious customers, or competitors who may want to put us out of business. To naively imagine that such risks are remote or don't apply to us is to live in the minefield of unawareness.

The demise of People Express airline is a case in point. The airline's founder and executive corps believed passengers flocked to People Express for low fares. Indeed, the airline did grow dramatically because of its low-fare approach. Rapid growth, however, soon eroded service. Management was caught unaware that the airline's customers valued a minimal level of service, as much as they valued low fares. When the service level dropped below that minimum, customers switched to other airlines. Management missed the opportunity to institute a modest fare increase to raise the service level and save the company.

Consider the case of James, a new building contractor. He is handy with tools and great at shopping for bargains among suppliers. However, he believes he has sufficient knowledge of the building codes to operate his venture without risk. In reality, he is largely ignorant of the complexities of the codes. His days as an entrepreneur are numbered. For James, a huge step in the right direction would be to admit his lack of knowledge. The next step would be to hold back on pursuing the contracting business while he either (1) studies the codes, ideally with an experienced contractor or other professional in the trade, or (2) hires or contracts with someone who is knowledgeable in this area.

HOW AWARE ARE YOU *RIGHT NOW?*

Detached observation happens in the present—*right now*, not five minutes ago or tonight or tomorrow morning. If you are fretting over past deeds or are preoccupied with next week's billings or next month's client prospect, you are *not* in the present. Listen to Ken Robert's novel *A Rich Man's Secret*, the musings of Clement Watt in a letter addressed "Dear friend": "Cease worrying about who you were, and who you may someday become. Bury the dead Past, and trust not the Future. *Stay here.* Rarely will you meet a person who is Here. Most are sadly lost to regrets about the past, and fears of the future, lost to the ordinary, anxious thoughts that imperil our existence. Only by staying *here* can you ever change."

Don't wonder what you might learn in the steps to come; stay with this book line for line and thought for thought. And as you move through each step, apply what Step 1 taught you about awareness. Awareness is, in fact, the basic tool to construct your business. Keep it handy; use it often.

Awareness brings that lazy, half-sleeping part of you to life. You will then be in that tiny minority of people who stop sleepwalking through life and actually realize what they are doing while they are doing it—and how their actions affect others around them.

Sir Isaac Newton, when graced with a dazzling experience of awareness, said it this way: "I seem to have been only like a boy playing on the seashore, and diverting myself in now and then finding a smoother pebble or a prettier shell than ordinary, whilst the great ocean of truth lay all undiscovered before me." Imagine—one of the greatest inventors, scientists, and mathematicians considered his accomplishments like "playing on the seashore" compared with the truths he began to perceive when he awoke to the brilliance of awareness!

LINK YOUR AWARENESS AND YOUR EXPERIENCE

Awareness develops, in part, from experience. Successful businesspeople speak highly of "business experience." Experience is the history of events in a particular sector and what an individual has learned through those events. The more events you observe or participate in, the more experience you have. Let us be aware, however, that going through an event—such as working for someone who has to declare bankruptcy—does not guarantee that we have learned all we need to know from that event. It is possible to participate and observe and yet have only shallow awareness. Actively deepening your awareness, however, will guarantee that you stand a much better chance of not repeating a mistake.

A vast database of experiences gives you rich resources from which to draw when making business decisions. The more experiences you have in your memory with which to compare a present difficulty or opportunity, the more likely it is that you will make an effective decision.

That is why review organizations such as community college small business centers, fee-based small business consulting services, and SCORE (Service Corps of Retired Executives, a part of the Small Business Administration) can be such huge assets to people who are relatively new to business. Such services help entrepreneurs struggling for a firm footing to bring to the table many databases of experiences from different sectors. A new business owner who "can't bother" with putting his or her data through a review by experienced professionals passes up a tremendous opportunity to fine-tune the venture, and perhaps spot and head off some threat looming on the horizon.

Among the reasons a small business owner may be reluctant to submit the business to a review are:

- *Mental or emotional laziness.* "It's just too much trouble; we're doing OK the way we are."
- *Fear of criticism.* Denial may tell the entrepreneur that outside review is unnecessary. The unexpressed fear is: "They'll shoot me down. I don't want to go through the embarrassment of having people with so much expertise nitpick my business to death."
- *Fear of taking on the work of serious business-building.* Again, most likely this would not be expressed in a forthright fashion. The subconscious of the person in denial here might wish to say: "I know there are problems, but it's easier just not understanding how serious they are.

It'll be too much sweat to fix my attitudes and my ways of doing business to match up to what perceptive former executives might establish as an agenda for change."

Awareness, in any of the above cases, would uncover the denial—and lay the foundation for a summoning of courage and energy to overcome the laziness or the fears. Let me be perfectly clear about saying that awareness will not solve the problem. Without awareness, though, it is extremely unlikely that the entrepreneur will move forward through the steps defined and explained in this book that are necessary for successful change and growth.

Like a light that banishes the darkness from a room, awareness brightens up and casts light around all corners of your business. The brighter the light, the more you will illuminate the areas of your business that still lie in the shadows.

Do not imagine that you can detach the development or evolution of awareness in your business life from your awareness of life in general. It works much better, in fact, the other way around. If you are aware of the simple, ordinary facets of your everyday existence—learn to really *see* them, *hear* them, *feel* them—you position yourself to heighten your awareness of what is going on in, and around, your business. Pause then for a moment to consider something very ordinary: your act of reading this book.

Where are you *right now* in your consciousness of what you are doing, and how you are reacting? Notice the book in your hands: its weight, the texture of the paper, the look of the type on the pages. Move your awareness to your body posture *at this moment:* Are you slouching or squirmy or sitting up squarely and comfortably? Feel your weight pressing against the chair or couch. Feel any tension that may be present in your body. Now become aware of your breathing: Is it calm, irregular, or heavy? Take a few deliberate deep breaths. What are your thoughts and feelings *right now?* Answer these questions aloud. Do the answers sound as if you're aware or in denial? Repeat the exercise until you feel you are in the *now* and *aware.*

I am not talking about evaluating or judging here. Yes, evaluating and judging are important skills in the running of a business. You will need such skills to guesstimate with a fair degree of accuracy the likelihood of a particular outcome in product development, sales, marketing, or customer relations. But right here, right now, I am talking about simply observing what is going on, both inside yourself and inside your business. Do not assign any value of good or bad, congratulate yourself for something that seems to be a positive or castigate yourself (or others) for what might seem to be off track. This exercise is difficult because we are so accustomed to making judgments of everything that swims into our consciousness, especially if it has an impact on our business venture. Nonetheless, please trust me when I say that acquiring this facility of being a neutral observer is *extremely* important if you are to move toward productive change in your business and in your life.

What could you observe right now about the current state of your business? I invite you to pause here and make a short list of characteristics of your business, relationships (both internal and external), and the atmosphere in which you go about your workday. A hypothetical sample list might say something like: We are an office supplies store, located in the heart of the business district of a small southeastern city. We stock 1,015 different products. We employ 5 people full-time and 12 part-time. Our carpeting is blue and somewhat frayed, and our walls and ceiling are a cream color. We have windows that give us natural light and look out on a busy

> ▪▪▪▪▪
> What can you observe about your business and relationships? Write your list in the lines below:
> _____
> _____
> _____
> _____
> _____
> _____
> _____
> _____

street. Most of our customers come from a radius of 12 miles and are predominantly male. We have relationships with about 30 different suppliers."

HOW DO YOU RESIST BEING AWARE?

Awareness is the foundation upon which all the other steps in mastering the small business challenge are built. Resistance to awareness—especially in our extroverted, fast-paced culture—is more the norm than the exception. You may find yourself wanting to resist it because it feels too simple, too childish, or just not relevant to what you want to accomplish.

If you find that you are resisting reading about and practicing awareness, *be aware of your resisting*—both feelings and thoughts. Once you see what you are dealing with, then you can acknowledge your resistance—and move forward.

Have you ever stopped smoking? Or deliberately changed your wardrobe? Or decided you were tired of paying rent and saved to purchase a house? All of these changes required awareness. What I want to do here is make you aware of your own awareness. And aware of how awareness functions as a foundation for change.

Think for a moment of things that you have consciously changed in yourself in the past few years: your habits, your lifestyle, or your way of running your life. Notice, as you mull over these things in your mind, how you became aware of the need to make a change, and how that awareness began to motivate you.

> Write some examples of your instances of awareness and the changes that resulted from them:
> _____
> _____
> _____
> _____
> _____
> _____

Ask yourself, "In my type of business, what are the extremely productive and successful owner-managers aware of that I am not? If they are bigger, better capitalized, and positioned to take a much larger slice of the market than I am, what makes this so?"

While capital is indeed important, there are many examples of people starting with relatively little money and developing powerful and cash-rich businesses. So the mere fact that some competitors may have begun with more capital behind them than you is not enough to explain the difference between the evolution of their operation and yours.

So . . . what are others in your field aware of that you have been overlooking or minimizing?

Let us look in for a moment on Frank.

Frank runs a small print shop. He knows about desktop publishing, short-run printing, stocking the right supplies, and dealing well with his three employees and his customers. But Frank's list of what he doesn't know very well includes marketing, competitive analysis, and business strategies. No wonder Frank's print shop has stayed small. If he doesn't know about or act on these areas, it is unlikely he will grow—or even stay competitive.

Making the list jolts Frank into awareness. Now he can decide what to do about sizing up the competition in the vicinity and the way it is affecting his business—and also what he has to do in order to keep abreast of the technological evolution in short-run printing.

Frank is especially struck, however, by the realization that he knows next to nothing about strategic planning for business growth. This new awareness drives him to enroll for a short course in this subject at the continuing education division of a nearby college. Frank now has an agenda for change.

What about you? Be aware of your strengths and weaknesses by filling out these two lists:

What I know and do well in my business:

_____
_____
_____
_____
_____
_____

Things I need to know and skills in which I'm weak:

_____
_____
_____
_____
_____
_____

WAYS TO BECOME MORE AWARE

Meditation is a powerful tool for increasing awareness. Meditation teaches you to observe and become more aware of everything that is inside of you. You learn to sit back and observe everything, mostly your thoughts and feelings, as they race by in the moment-by-moment reality that is your life.

If you already practice a form of meditation, keep it up—you are definitely on the right track! If you have not begun to devote time to meditating, consider starting. It will make a difference in how you create your life—and your business.

Whether you meditate or not, you will be able to appreciate this example. Recall the last time you switched from driving one model of car to another model, perhaps by an entirely different manufacturer. Let's say you had been accustomed to driving a sedate sedan and suddenly you switched to a sports car. Probably before you took the plunge you had not been aware of how many sports cars were on the road with you. Within a week or two of buying your own sports car—maybe even from the moment you started to think of owning one—you started to notice an amazing number of sports cars. Had the market suddenly become flooded with sports cars? No! The change took place inside you—in a fresh awareness of the number of sports cars on the road.

Similarly, when you got into business, you became aware that the world was not made up solely of "working stiffs," that there were, indeed, substantial numbers of people out on their own, people who woke each morning with a different set of parameters for the day from the folks who work 9-to-5. In leaving the world of the "securely" employed, you set your own agenda.

Notice things around you. Be aware! Today or tomorrow, note how many things you had been walking past without seeing them. Perhaps the ornate scrollwork on the cornices of vintage buildings, or the cheerful smile on the face of that bubbly waitress at the coffee shop. Think, for a moment, of the truth behind this aphorism by G. K. Chesterton: "The things we see every day are the things we never see at all."

A great way to expand your awareness is to work with a partner. For example—reading this book with a partner, exchanging ideas as you go, step by step, will probably increase the book's impact by at least 30 percent on each of you. Talking over ideas with another person will almost always expand awareness—even if all you learn is what you *don't* want to do! Each of you has different insights, and sharing them makes you both get deeper below the surface.

Now that you have learned to increase your awareness—you are ready to proceed to Step 2, "Harness the Positive Power of Attention." We'll focus your awareness and apply it to specific situations. Stay alert—sharp bends in the road just ahead!

TEST YOUR INNER GAME EQ: AWARENESS

Rate yourself from 1 (weak) to 5 (strong) on how much each statement reflects your current state. Go with the first answer that comes to mind as you read each statement. Circle the number that best represents your capacity in each quiz item.

1. I am aware of awareness.   1 2 3 4 5
2. I can stay in the present moment.   1 2 3 4 5
3. I am able to observe from a
   detached state.   1 2 3 4 5
4. I notice my self-talk.   1 2 3 4 5
5. I work to expand my awareness.   1 2 3 4 5

Awareness total _____

Harness the Positive Power of Attention

Do what you are doing while you are doing it.
—A Zen principle

Attention is closely linked to awareness. As your awareness develops and deepens, so will your capacity to pay close attention to things. If awareness acts like a light illuminating the darkness, attention gives you the ability to direct that light where you choose.

The light beam we are calling "attention" can not only be directed, it can also be focused and concentrated. You can zero in on the details that matter most.

Often people call focused attention "concentration." In this step I'll help you measure the degree of concentration you currently exercise, and show you how to increase it. I'll also explain the many benefits of increased concentration on growing your business.

Try this little experiment. Can you feel your blood moving through your veins? No? Try again. Stop everything else you are doing or thinking about—and concentrate. *Focus your attention* on your left wrist. Can you feel your pulse?

That's your blood coursing along. So, when you truly concentrate, you can indeed feel your blood.

What's the point? Simply put, there is great value for you personally and for your business in being able to thus focus your attention. Many who fail in their small business ventures fail because they haven't learned to pay attention.

The word "attention" comes from two Latin words: *ad* meaning "toward," and *tendere* meaning "to stretch." So when you focus your attention on something, you "stretch toward it." When you pay attention, you learn. Attention allows you to tackle a host of complex tasks—such as a multifaceted strategic planning program—that otherwise would seem daunting. *Paying attention pays off.*

Attention is a bit like breathing—everybody does it, nobody really notices it. *False!* Not everybody "does" attention very well, and if you do have it down, believe me you will notice it. When we really pay attention, *we realize we are paying attention.*

Attention is so taken for granted that it is easy to overlook its benefits. In my experience, the main benefits of focusing your attention well are these:

- Greater productivity
- Better results
- More clarity
- Higher creativity
- Improved learning

Aren't these precisely the qualities that build a successful business? Mark and Jocelyn have certainly found this to be true. They specialize in engraving and silkscreening—everything from caps to jackets to trophies to you-name-it.

Engraving demands precision. And first-rate time management skills. You can't dawdle all day over one coffee mug.

On the other hand, every engraving you do absolutely must look great. Thus, their challenge has been to organize the production of precision products with mass-produced efficiency. Without finely focused attention, they would not have been able to produce quality engraving in a fast-moving production process, and grow their cottage industry.

GET IN THE FLOW

Focusing your thoughts and energy on an idea or project is what makes the project happen! You can conceptualize it as the flow of the jet stream that builds to a certain power and pushes the aircraft into the air.

Flow is that state of highly focused but *relaxed* attention. When you are in this state, you have great powers of concentration. Your mind, however, is not tense but generally relaxed. In effect, the state is one of calm focus. These qualities—being calm and being focused—might seem at first to be opposites, but in flow they coexist harmoniously. The relaxed state comes from confidence gained by being very well trained and prepared. This is a relatively new concept in the reaching for high performance states. Better understood and developed in the world of sports, the concept nonetheless has important applications for small business owners.

The study of flow was begun by professor Mihaly Csikszentmihalyi (pronounced Chik-SENT-mi-hy) at the University of Chicago some 20 years ago. Far from just an academic discipline, however, flow has been applied to a tremendous variety of human activities already, from creation of curriculum design to new product development and leisure services to the training of managers. Research, meanwhile, has gone global.

"Some people," Csikszentmihalyi reports in his 1990 book *Flow: The Psychology of Optimal Experience,* "learn to use this priceless resource efficiently, while others waste it. The mark of a person who is in control of consciousness is the ability to focus attention at will, to be oblivious to distractions, to concentrate for as long as it takes to achieve a goal, and not longer."

He quotes a dancer describing how it feels when a performance is going well: "Your concentration is very complete. Your mind isn't wandering, you are not thinking of something else; you are totally involved in what you are doing. . . . Your energy is flowing very smoothly. You feel relaxed, comfortable, and energetic."

Picture a figure skater in world-class competition. She has practiced her jumps and spins thousands of times. Now, in the bright glow of the arena lights, with millions of people watching, she has to "ace" her jumps, landing each time with grace and poise. She totally lets go of her anxieties and fears and lets her body soar into the air on the strength of her confident *knowing* that she has executed the routine flawlessly in practice, and there is no reason why she can't do it again before the crowd. To the amazement of the crowd, the skater makes each of three daring leaps and lands beautifully, with full balance, on a single blade. She's in the flow!

The state of concentrated but relaxed attention called flow has many natural applications for entrepreneurs. Most obviously, flow has great benefits for people engaged in developing a marketing campaign, including designing ads and commercials; creating a business strategy for the coming year; or putting together, and then delivering, a sales presentation.

In the powerful, expansive mode of flow, fear of failure recedes to practically zero. All matters not bearing on the activity of the moment are pushed far to the periphery of the mind, if not obliterated entirely. A person's whole mental, emotional, and psychic energy is brought to bear on delivering the best performance possible. What a state of mind in which to make a sales call! Or lead a staff meeting. Or produce the final draft of a report. Or whatever activity you can imagine that will bear on the success of your enterprise.

Can you recollect some instances when you felt "in the flow" (either in a business activity, learning a new skill, or in an athletic contest)? What did that feel like?

> Describe how being in the flow affected your feelings and your performance:
> _____
> _____
> _____
> _____
> _____
> _____

TIES BETWEEN AWARENESS AND ATTENTION

Awareness is a prerequisite for attention. There is a fair amount of overlap between the two, and yet it is important to distinguish one skill from the other. Perhaps the concepts of "overall" and "specific" are the most helpful in making the distinction. *Awareness,* remember, is that broad wash of light that illuminates a general area, whereas *attention* is concentrating that light like the beam of a flashlight so that a very specific spot is lit up brightly and fine details can be observed.

Consider communication skills. "When I talk, people listen—and they really pick up on what I'm saying. I get results!" proclaims Sally Ann, who is proud of herself for becoming a leader in her metro area in computer software training and Web site design and management. At the same time, her staff and many of her clients are fuming because while Sally Ann does a lot of talking, she seldom listens well, or takes other people's input or feedback seriously. Because Sally Ann isn't aware of her true communication style, she can't pay attention to the right things, and can't experience the benefits of being in the flow.

Awareness might dawn upon Sally Ann one day when she sees the results of an anonymous inventory of staff attitudes, administered by an outside consultant. The survey shows, for example, that while she monopolizes meetings and lays down a heavy barrage of words, only a small percentage of her words are being translated into effective action by "the troops."

So, our software whiz has been hit by a broad wash of light. Once she is aware of her ineffective communication style, she can pay attention to how her communication style impacts her staff.

Let's see if we can break this down into the specifics that Sally Ann needs to identify and pay attention to. She needs to:

- *Listen first, then respond.* Sally Ann needs to put her own agenda in the background long enough to be able to really hear what her staff and her clients are saying. Then she needs to frame her replies in such a way that she takes their hopes, desires, fears, needs, and whatever else she's hearing, into active consideration.

- *Practice active listening.* Active listening requires concentration and giving encouraging feedback—paraphrasing the other speaker's message, for instance, without conveying any judgment: "Oh, I think I see, John. What you're trying to tell me is. . . ." Another technique is to mentally summarize for yourself what the other person is saying; this will help you forgo interrupting so you can paraphrase and also will keep you focused on what the person's message is. Make your mental summaries very brief so you don't miss what the person says next. You can think twice as fast as the other person is talking, and it is easy to use this extra speed to get distracted or to daydream. The mental summary technique helps you avoid this distraction and stay focused.
- *Employ body language that supports listening.* Maintain eye contact while you listen, nod to show that you are following, etc.
- *Ask information-seeking, not argumentative, questions.* "Carol, I don't understand why this new supplier would be better than our current supplier. Could you explain?"
- *Notice her own reactions to what other people are saying.* "Hmm. What Carol is saying makes me want to resist her suggestions to the hilt. Why do I feel so strongly that she's off base?"

Using these powerful techniques, you can bring your awareness to your conversations and focus your attention on the techniques so that you employ them effectively.

As you can now easily imagine, it is important to *be aware* of how well you do—or do not—listen. Recall right now the instances where you believe you listened well, and why you were able to do so. Recall also those times when you were distracted and listened poorly—and why.

▪▪▪▪▪
Times I listened well:
_____
_____
_____
_____
_____

▪▪▪▪▪
Times I listened poorly:
_____
_____
_____
_____
_____

RESOLVE CONFLICTS TO ENHANCE COMMUNICATION

To resolve conflicts effectively, apply the active listening tips in the previous section. And be aware that nobody is ever 100 percent right or wrong. A willingness to change your view is also part of good conflict resolution techniques. Open yourself up to be persuaded by the evidence or ideas presented by others—things that perhaps you had not taken into consideration. Or be prepared to answer others' objections by your own reasoned presentation.

We'll talk about feelings in Step 4, but let me mention here that being aware of your feelings while in the midst of a conflict is extremely important. This also will help you to develop a capacity to empathize with others. Once you feel what others are feeling—or, at least, get somewhere in the ballpark of their feelings—you will have the rapport with them you need to work toward a resolution of your differences.

"AMERICAMANIA" STOPS THE FLOW

"Americamania" is living in a hyperpaced environment as you grab fast food on the run and charge around in ten different directions during the course of a single day. If this sounds like your life, you need to regain your ability to pay attention so you can benefit from being in the flow.

Keep Your Attention Strong and Sharply Focused

Attention has two major components: (1) strength and (2) focus. Many times they go hand in hand: One who has strong (intense) powers of concentration will also be sharply focused (details come up sharply etched and glitches or flaws are clearly discernible). However, this is not always the case. It is possible to have strong but dispersed powers of concentration. Or, you may have the capacity to focus sharply but nonetheless lack intensity. Be aware of how you do or do not concentrate. You cannot improve your performance unless you know how you currently exercise your concentration. The following descriptions may help:

- *Weak attention is characterized by a lack of energy.* You know you should be concentrating on something—whether it is finding an accountant or writing job descriptions for the people you have hired. But you go at it half-heartedly, or you procrastinate indefinitely. Everyone has some problems with attention. But if you find yourself being "fuzzy on the details" on important matters—things that are vital to the viability of your venture—take heed! Failing to increase your power of attentive focusing may spell death for your business.
- *Weak attention can be traced to something as simple as lack of adequate exercise, poor nutrition, or other health problems.* See your health professionals—all of them. Get your eyes and hearing tested along with a full physical examination. If you suspect that you are a victim of mood swings, depression, or Attention Deficit Hyperactivity Disorder (ADHD)—a recent survey showed a high percentage of entrepreneurs are ADHD—seek out experts in these areas who can help you understand these conditions and get them under control. Ask family, friends, and coworkers for suggestions.
- *Your attention may not be so much weak as it is wandering.* This is a common problem. You are trying to bear down on an important marketing campaign, but every time you start working on it, your attention is diverted by other problems or projects (business or personal). Learning prioritizing and other time-management skills may help solve this problem. Effective delegating also may help. Put more energy into concentrating on aspects of your business, one at a time. You can learn to focus more sharply.

The following steps will heighten your concentration:

- *Improve your diet.* Reduce saturated fats and refined-sugar-based products. Increase consumption of whole grains, nuts, raw vegetables, and healthy protein.
- *Start (and continue) a well-balanced exercise program.*
- *Use your mind regularly.* Enjoy challenging reading and discussions. Avoid passive TV watching.
- *Practice daily meditation.* Choose your technique, there are many available.

Make your choices—and follow through!

Mental decline and loss of emotional energy can be reversed through improved nutrition and sleep habits, and through a healthy program of exercise. "The fight," says Dr. George A. Sheehan, a New Jersey cardiologist who writes regularly on the benefits of jogging, ". . . is never with age; it is with boredom, with routine, with the danger of not living at all." If we give in to negative patterns, he suggests, "life will stop, growth will cease, learning will come to an end."

The simplest things can make a difference. For instance, few of us drink enough *water!* Drink a glass of water four or five times a day—especially just before an activity that requires intense concentration. Water works like a fuel additive for gasoline—it heightens performance. The same seems to be true of rhythmic breathing. Stop what you are doing periodically and engage in deliberate deep breathing. Breathe deeply, hold your breath for five or ten seconds, then expel the breath. Do this for three or four minutes at a time. Your brain will thrive on the extra oxygen it receives through this exercise and will reward you with an improved capacity for concentration.

How does noise affect you? For some, the hum of traffic rising from the street below the office is music to the ears, as may be the occasional sounds of footsteps in the corridors or in adjacent offices. For others, it is better to muffle such sounds by playing music. Some people would go crazy if they had to try to concentrate with rock or country music playing in the background; others would go to sleep to the strains of classical music. Experiment to find what works best for you and your staff. But remember, the goal is *increased production.*

Attention and Work Styles

Most of us have read an article or two from research into the differences in work styles among people of different personality types, ages, or cultural backgrounds. Few, however, take these articles as seriously as we should. This time, pay attention!

Among the variances you should note in your own and others' styles of performing work are:

- Peak hours
- Pace
- Duration
- People contact
- Project variety
- Distraction tolerance

Let's go through each point briefly.

Peak hours. People have natural cycles that govern their attention capacities. Your ability to focus, in other words, fluctuates during the day. These cycles are different from one person to another. Thus, when you are pouring all your energy and focus into a project, others around you may be less able to do so *at that time.*

Each person has a certain time of day when he or she is at peak focusing power. It could literally be any time around the clock. Some people like to rise as early as 3 or 4 AM because that is the best time for directing their energies. When are you at your best? If you've never thought about it carefully until just this moment, think about it *now!* List an actual time span, such as 6 to 8 AM, or 3 to 6 PM, or whatever. Few people seem to be at their best just after lunch. It's usually better to conduct serious conferencing or problem solving before noon or after 2 PM.

If you're bringing a team together for a project, choose an hour for your work session when at least the majority of the team members are in an area that is either their peak or their second best period for concentration. And be forgiving if one or another member is "out of synch" because the time you've chosen is less than ideal for those individuals.

■■■■■
My peak (optimum) hours for getting work done are:
_____

■■■■■
The peak hours for my key associates or team members are:

Name _____ Peak hours _____

Name _____ Peak hours _____

Name _____ Peak hours _____

Name _____ Peak hours _____

Name _____ Peak hours _____

Pace. Some people seem to rush from one task to another as if there were no tomorrow. Get in their way and you risk being run over. To suggest to these folks that they slow down is like uttering an abominable heresy.

At the other end of the spectrum are the plodders. "Easy does it!" is their slogan. Their slow, methodical pace can resemble a turtle crawl. To try to push these people into working at a faster pace is to invite their wrath and alienation.

The important thing to note here is that one pace is not necessarily, or always, better than another. Each has its own advantages and drawbacks, and its own time and place. But taking your own natural pace and that of others with whom you work into consideration as you plan your activities is a matter of great common sense.

Duration. How long can you effectively concentrate on any one project? An hour? Two? More? How about the people you work with? Often, we reach a point of diminishing returns after an hour or so of intense concentration (such as a problem-solving meeting).

Closely related is the subject of needed time away from a project. Hence, the expression, "Let's sleep on it." Often the best thing you can do is go out and play golf or go to a movie, then get back to tackling your problem later. Taking a break could also mean switching your focus to another project for awhile, then returning to the first one later in the day.

Again, *know thyself!* Figure out what works best for you—and do it.

People contact. The degree of people contact suitable for each of us constitutes a major work style. Many entrepreneurs prefer—or even seem to "need"—a substantial amount of people contact. But this is not true for all. There are those who work best if they can work entirely alone. For such individuals, too much people contact is a huge distraction and a headache.

Quite a few of us have needs that seem like opposites: We may thrive on people contact up to a point, but then require sizable doses of solitude. It's the going back and forth between people contact and quiet isolation that brings out our best creative energies. What is true for you?

> My best work style in terms of people contact and/or solitude is: _____
> _____

Project variety. Are you so single-minded that you can only work on one project over an extended time period—a morning, a day, a week? Would going back and forth among two or three different things within a short time span be difficult or wearing for you? If so, you had better tailor your work to that mode.

Most people can handle a limited number of projects in the course of a day. But how many do you believe you can manage effectively? Often, entrepreneurs must learn the art of juggling. It seems to be the nature of the beast. It helps, though, to have a fair idea of the number of balls you can keep in the air at one time. Can you work on quarterly taxes, run a meeting on sales tips for your staff, deal with the computer-repair service person, and still remember to order flowers for a friend in the hospital—all in one morning? Some people can, some can't. Again, knowing what you can handle is what's important, and you had better learn your limits or you will never find the time to take your venture to the next level.

Distraction tolerance. Distractions, changes, and interruptions are part of everyday life in business. Or anywhere, for that matter. Some of us, however, tolerate distractions much better than others. If you are someone for whom "the least little thing" is likely to disrupt your focus on the activity at hand, you may want to work with a counselor or a coach about increasing your capacity to put up with interruptions and disappointments. Once again, the main thing is to know just what your tolerances are. If you find you need to isolate yourself from others, at least for parts of the day, do so. A telephone answering service entrepreneur I know has become much more productive in managing his business since he leased a separate small office across the hall from where his staff of ten works. Previously, he had been within earshot of all their conversations with callers, and had been badly hampered in his ability to get his work done.

DEVELOP A KEY MEASURE

Sometimes attention is something you need to spread out over an extended period—maybe a week or a month—even a year. In other words, you need to pay attention to a trend, or to your progress toward achieving a goal, such as a 15 percent increase in sales.

In these cases what works amazingly well is what I call a "key measure." This is any technique or method that can translate into a number (or even better, a statistic) that you can track. A key measure will allow you to gauge just how well you are focused and moving ahead on a plan or a project—or how close you are to achieving a goal.

Tracking receipts or prospect calls or the conversion rate of sales calls to actual sales are good key measures. Visual displays, such as charts or graphs, work well to represent key measures. One common visual display for people working on complex projects, such as constructing a house or a commercial building, is called a "Gantt chart." Along the bottom of such a chart you would run a time line for the whole project, from start to finish. Along the left-hand margin, you would put the major components: sewer, foundation, frame, roof, plumbing, etc.

Use all the good key measures and displays you can muster. Better than any other device you could imagine, they will keep you focused on how your business is progressing—and show you where your weak spots are.

Now that you have mastered awareness and attention, Step 3 will take you on a tour of your own mind. What's stored up there? How do those programs affect how you think and act?

TEST YOUR INNER GAME EQ: ATTENTION

Rate yourself from 1 (weak) to 5 (strong) on how much each statement reflects your current state. Go with the first answer that comes to mind as you read each statement. Circle the number that best represents your capacity in each quiz item.

1. I am aware of attention.   1 2 3 4 5
2. I am able to focus my attention. 1 2 3 4 5
3. I notice my level of concentration. 1 2 3 4 5
4. I am aware and use my attention/work styles. 1 2 3 4 5
5. I am improving my attention skills. 1 2 3 4 5

Attention total _____

Recognize Mind-Sets That Help or Hurt Your Company

> It is the mind that makes good or ill, that maketh wretch or happy, rich or poor.
> —Edmund Spenser

Prior to 1954, scientists—and many of the world's best runners—thought that it was not possible for a human being to run a mile in less than four minutes. A gazelle or a cheetah, yes; a man or a woman, no. Even the *New England Journal of Medicine* and other medical publications put out research that "proved" that this was so. Then in 1954 Roger Bannister of England broke four minutes running the mile. A physician himself, Bannister had an intuition that the human body was indeed capable of such a feat. And he proved it with his own two legs.

While Bannister's record is well known, what is much less known is that 37 other runners were able to run the mile in under four minutes over the next 12 months, and many of them beat Bannister's time! After so many years of runners attempting unsuccessfully to break the four-minute mile, what happened to change things? Did the human body suddenly get that much stronger? Not at all. What happened was that one man's "doing the impossible" rewrote the mental model that had, in effect, been governing the cultural mind-sets, or beliefs, of the worlds of athletics and of biological scientists. Popular mind-sets were changed, and what had widely been thought unattainable all at once became possible.

Impeding mind-sets have major implications for developing companies. Self-fulfilling prophecies, such as "I'm not very good with money," or "We're doing OK, but we'll probably never be a very large operation," or "The world's a crazy place, we're just trying to keep our heads above water," or "It's hard to find good help," or "You just can't trust people anymore," govern the fate of many a small enterprise. Henry Ford said: "Whether you think you can or you think you can't, you're right." Stephen Covey came along several generations after Ford and put it differently: "The way we see the problem is the problem."

We all harbor mind-sets—actually hundreds of them—and they set the limits for us on how we believe we can perform, or on what we believe we can accomplish. Our mind-sets, or mental models, put filters on how we see the world, and how we make sense of it.

Are you hearing yourself anywhere in here? In other words, what limits have you been placing on yourself as you develop your venture? Are you saying to yourself, "I've got to keep our advertising costs down," or "No way I want to deal with more than five employees," or *what?* And, equally important, where have those limits come from?

HOW MIND-SETS AFFECT YOUR PERCEPTIONS

Did you hear the following things about money when you were a child? Put a check mark next to those that you recognize as very familiar:

❏ Don't put that in your mouth. Money is dirty.

❏ We might not be rich, but we have our health.

- ❏ Money is the root of all evil.
- ❏ Save your money for a rainy day.
- ❏ Money doesn't grow on trees.
- ❏ When I was your age we were so poor I had to . . .
- ❏ A penny saved is a penny earned.
- ❏ It takes money to make money.
- ❏ Is that money burning a hole in your pocket?
- ❏ The rich keep getting richer.
- ❏ You work all day, and what do you get? Another day older and deeper in debt.

Let's see what other money mind-sets you bring to your venture by completing this list. Some expressions regarding money I remember from my childhood:

_____

_____

_____

_____

The above exercise represents an informal exploration of just one mental model that influences your approach to running your venture. Remember that there are many, many more. Mental models have overriding impact on whether we:

- See ourselves as attractive to others—either for our physical appearance or our way of dealing with people (and hence, "salable").
- Operate in an organized or a disorganized fashion.
- Are able to ask for help from experts in various areas where we are weak.
- Manage to get along with a spouse or business partner or our staff.
- Can judge when it is reasonable to take a risk—and how much of a risk to take.

As you have surely realized as you read this, these are *critical* factors in the evolution of a small business. It is important, therefore, that you (1) become very *aware* of your mind-sets and (2) turn your attention, like a powerful flashlight beam, on those that may be holding you back from achieving your goals.

Mind-sets, or mental models, are beliefs about a particular subject area or a situation. If I am walking alone at night on a dark street and two hulky young men are walking toward me, I will cross to the other side of the street (mind-set—hulky young men on the streets at night can be dangerous). Mind-sets are a viewpoint, a way of seeing an element of reality. Psychologists and sociologists also use other terms of mind-sets, terms such as "perceptions" or "filters" or "reality tunnels."

Whatever you call them, mind-sets strongly influence how you live your life and the types of experiences you have. You do not simply take in reality on a blank screen. Your mind is already jammed full of preconceptions, judgments, or understandings, and when you are confronted with exterior reality to assimilate, you do so through the filters of what you already believe. There are actually four parts to this process:

1. *You look out on the world and perceive what is going on:* New person is approaching my desk, traffic is massing up ahead on the freeway, an unexpected problem report is landing in my in-tray, etc.
2. *You associate what you perceive with what is in your database of experience:* New people put an extra demand on my energy—introductions and all. I've been in too many traffic jams on this road before, this'll probably be rough and tie me up for an hour. Problem reports mean more work—not fun!
3. *Only after you associate with past experience do you evaluate:* Wait, this new person looks friendly and unassuming; I might even enjoy meeting her. Let's see, this is either an accident ahead or road work or the early comers to the big basketball game at the arena tonight. Well, this report isn't very thick, maybe this won't be as bad as the last one.
4. *You make a decision about how to handle the situation:* I'm going to smile and say "hello." No sense stewing; I'm not late for anything; may as well enjoy the jazz on the radio. I think I'll drop what I've been doing and plunge into this report right away. Maybe I can get started on a solution.

MIND-SETS, OR MENTAL MODELS, FILTER REALITY

Mental models serve to shape the rules that you follow to manage your life. These rules, like most rules, allow you to manage your life more effectively—for the most part. Some rules that served you well as a child, however, actually need to be broken or modified if you are to succeed as an adult entrepreneur. One example is the rule: Don't talk to strangers.

This rule is useful and important for children to know and follow. However, it can hinder the development of your business, especially if it is dependent on networking or cold calling.

Mind-sets are like mental habits. Because they are mental habits, they are much harder to notice, and therefore, to change. To change your outdated mental models, you first have to notice them—to be aware that they exist—and then you must focus your attention on them persistently until you achieve the change you desire.

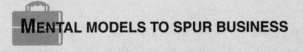

MENTAL MODELS TO SPUR BUSINESS

Most successful business people share some mind-sets with others who have achieved their goals. Some of these mind-sets are:

1. I can learn from everything that happens to me or around me.

2. I retain my power when I take responsibility for my actions.

3. I am more productive when I focus on solutions rather than on problems.

4. I learn from my mistakes.

5. I fail only when I stop trying.

6. I share credit with others who have been part of a successful effort.

7. My limits are largely self imposed—and I can change them.

Another metaphor for thinking about mental models is as maps. Maps take a complex area and represent it in small patches, and in a simpler form. By land or by sea, it's much easier to navigate with a map.

Outdated mental models are a particular problem. Imagine yourself visiting a foreign city you had never been to before and trying to find your way around with a map that was 30 years old. You probably would have a fair amount of trouble: whole streets and squares would have been changed, some buildings torn down, others built since your map was drawn. What you need is a current map. The same is true for mind-sets.

The main reason that mental models are so powerful is that they filter what we see in the world, and bring it into our consciousness as refracted by our previous experiences—which created the thought patterns upon which we rely for guidance. Most people believe they see the world as it actually is. This is not the case. What we see is the world as we *believe* it is.

As an example, residents of a New England town spent many years drinking water that had been contaminated by underground pollution without perceiving that the water was weakening them physically. Only when their perceptions of reality were brought in line with the objective state of the polluted drinking water did they stop drinking the water and change their water system. The realization that they were poisoning themselves daily was what provided the catalyst for a change in the mind-sets of those townspeople.

Your mind-sets, mental models, or—more simply—beliefs, largely control your experience of life. Whether you see your life as a delight or drudgery depends mainly on your perceptions. This is not a new understanding. Back in 438 BC, Euripides wrote, "I have found power in the mysteries of thought." And Marcus Aurelius added this nuance: "If you are pained by external things, it is not they that disturb you, but your own judgment of them. And it is in your power to wipe out that judgment now." Most comforting of all, however, is what Victor Frankl, a Nazi concentration camp survivor, wrote in his book *Man's Search for Meaning:* ". . . everything can be taken from a man but one thing: The last of his freedoms—to choose one's attitude in any given set of circumstances, to choose one's way."

WHERE DO YOU GET THOSE MIND-SETS?

As a three-year-old, you probably paid great homage to "the big people" in your life—your parents, perhaps your daycare teacher, and other adults in your environment. Everything these "big people" told you was etched deeply into your impressionable mind.

Your mother said, "This is a chair." You repeated, "chair." Your father said, "Over here, this is a table." You parroted, "table." "Great!" they said, "You are a fast learner." Then your father said, "Remember, money is the root of all evil." And you repeated, "Money is the root of all evil." Your mother showed you a doll and said, "This is a doll." And you echoed, "doll." Then she said, "Be careful not to get your clothes dirty." And you said to yourself, "I mustn't get my clothes dirty."

These examples demonstrate how you learned as a child. They also suggest that what you learned was a mixture of fact and opinion. Except nobody taught you the difference between the two. Your father and your mother and your teachers didn't say, "I believe that money is the root of all evil." They just said it the way they told you that that four-legged wooden object against the wall was a "chair." So you learned with equal weight that "this is a chair" and "money is the root of all evil." No one brought up then that that was a misquotation from the Bible, which says, "The *love of money* is the root of all evil." (I Timothy 6:10). Consequently, much of your adult life has had to be spent examining your beliefs and sorting out which ones serve you well, and which ones do not.

Remember: Mind-sets take root through repetition. Just hearing something once usually will not have an overbearing influence on your future thought patterns. Hearing messages over and over is what etches them deeply into your subconscious. The good news is that your mental models can be changed through repetition as well.

HOW YOUR MIND-SETS AFFECT YOUR BUSINESS STRATEGY

Your mental models shape your business viewpoint and strategy. If you were taught to reach for the stars, and you really bought into that message, that's what you will do. If you were taught to always be very, very careful and don't stick your neck out too far, then you will be fairly allergic to the kinds of risk-taking that are necessary for dynamic business growth.

So . . . what were you taught? Below, write any key proverbs, aphorisms, principles, etc., that your parents, teachers, and others influential adults told you—and that you feel you accepted:

_____

_____

_____

Did you learn that people are basically good, honest, trustworthy, and reliable? Or did you hear they are bad, dishonest, untrustworthy, and unreliable? Did you learn to be extremely wary of the opposite sex? All of these mind-sets can greatly affect how you get along with partners, customers, employees, and suppliers. If you think being the boss means you don't have to worry about such things, ask yourself if you would willingly work with or for, or patronize, someone who doesn't trust or like you.

The mental models on which you operate your life also, obviously, affect your moods. One of the Apollo astronauts, for example, had a meteoric career and was one of the 12 men who walked on the moon. After his space travels, life became very hard for this astronaut. He got divorced and found himself struggling with both alcohol and depression. After years of therapy he discovered that he had been running his life on an unconscious rule: Each goal had to be bigger than the last. This is not an uncommon rule. Most people who have it seem to be able to cope well enough, but in this case, going to the moon was so overwhelming an accomplishment that suddenly, nothing else seemed to matter much as a goal.

If this astronaut's rule had been conscious, it would have been much easier to deal with. As a subconscious rule, however, all he saw were the rule's effects. It took real digging into his subconscious to ferret out the source of his depression.

Most of our mind-sets derive from other people's mind-sets—expressed to us as their opinions on life and work. Parents and teachers, as I have remarked, are especially significant to us as role models and probably have contributed the lion's share of our childhood-inculcated mind-sets. If we grow up with an open mind, we can see people and situations as they really are. If our mind is more or less closed, we see people and situations through filters that make it hard to deal with life realistically.

HOW YOU ALWAYS TRY TO BE "RIGHT"

Like everyone else, you want to have others validate your mind-sets, to tell you that what you believe in your deepest soul is "The Truth." Some psychologists call this system "the Thinker and the Prover." The Thinker part of you develops the mental models and ways of seeing the world. The Prover collects the data to back up the Thinker's beliefs.

Consider the Prover as a person walking through life carrying a bushel basket. Into the basket goes all evidence that supports the Thinker's understanding of reality. If the Thinker believes that Buicks are the only car to own, the Prover will be ever alert for positive anecdotes and statistics about Buicks to back up the Thinker's conviction. Evidence that doesn't do this will simply not make it into the basket.

As you mull over this Thinker and Prover model, search your memory for an instance when you already had a hard-and-fast opinion on something, then went around collecting evidence to confirm your opinion.

> Write down an opinion and the various pieces of evidence that you collected:
> _____
> _____
> _____
> _____
> _____

EVALUATING YOUR MENTAL MODELS

People tend to evaluate the ways they think as "good" or "bad," or possibly "true" or "false." In general, however, it's hard to call any model 100 percent true or right, or 100 percent false or wrong. For instance, say your mental model is "be careful." Well, there are times when that will help you and times when it may be to your disadvantage—when you may miss a great opportunity because you were too careful. Aristotelian logic is like a light switch: either "on" or "off"—in other words, "true" or "false." Your inner world is more like a dimmer or a volume switch. When you express opinions about yourself or others, it is more realistic to put things on a scale of one to ten. In this framework you might rate your chances a seven that if your team works overtime on a project, you'll beat the competition and win the contract. Don't guarantee it, however, and you may indeed work your tails off and still lose the contract, leaving everybody on your team demoralized.

Most of us—unfortunately—express our opinions as if they were factual and 100 percent true. We apply labels to other people, often in a somewhat prejudicial fashion, and imply that our labeling is as true as if we were to point at a chair and say, "This is a chair." Aristotelian logic—pretending everything is black or white—can cause collateral damage. Remember this the next time someone tries to get you to join in on "Andy's so lazy, it's just unreal," or "Betty Jean knows absolutely zip about how to do her job," or . . . , but you get the idea. No employee is either 100 percent lazy or 100 percent hard worker. Nobody knows everything about their job nor absolutely nothing about it.

A motivational consultant was asked to do some high performance work with the Los Angeles Dodgers. He started by asking each batter how much "on" he felt for hitting the ball, and told the players to reply using a scale of one to ten. If a player didn't give himself at least a seven, the consultant would do some motivating and energizing work with him to raise his readiness level. The Dodgers were happy with the results.

Another way to evaluate your mental models is to assess them as either effective or ineffective for what you are attempting to accomplish. For example, if you are taking early retirement and want to spend half of each weekday on the golf course or knee-deep in a trout stream, harboring a mind-set toward recreating to that degree would be entirely appropriate and "effective." It would be a much less effective mind-set to coddle if you were in the startup phase of running a roofing and siding business.

CHANGING YOUR MIND-SETS

Do you believe you can change your way of thinking? People often feel they cannot. "This is just the way I am" some say, or "Can't teach an old dog new tricks" or "Can't teach a fish to fly." Your entrepreneurial replacement mind-set would be, "I can change my mind by persistent effort. My ways of thinking are not set in stone." And neither are your ways of behaving. The perennial casual dresser can learn to dress well and present a professional appearance. A woman who has a lifelong allergy to keeping track of money can learn how to budget, save receipts, and balance her checkbook. These transitions may be difficult, but difficult is not the same as impossible.

You will recall we spent all of Step 2 learning to focus our attention. Now let's use this skill. We're going to discover the most ineffective mind-sets you harbor. They may begin with the words "I can't" or "It's extremely hard for me to. . . ." Samples: "I can't stand to think about taxes until a week before the filing deadline." "It's extremely hard for me to watch an employee work with any less fervor or dedication than I work myself."

> ▪▪▪▪▪
> My most ineffective mind-sets are:
> _____
> _____
> _____
> _____
> _____

Find the Source

Many times you can alter a mind-set simply by identifying its origin. "Oh, come to think of it, I had an uncle who hung around our house a lot and was always putting down teenagers who didn't have steady jobs. Maybe that's where my workaholic attitude began." Or: "In fifth grade, Mrs. Reisterdorf would always jump down the throat of any kid who asked what she considered 'a dumb question.' Maybe that's why I am always so afraid of asking questions during meetings."

If you consider yourself disorganized—or even outright sloppy—think back and see where this trait that you now consider a hindrance may have gotten its birth. Ditto for any prejudicial attitudes you can identify against people of the opposite sex, a different skin color, a different religion, or who speak with an accent. Be assured that you didn't become prejudiced all on your own. A prejudice is an acquired point of view.

To examine the source of each ineffective belief, or mind-set, is to bring the process of responding to mind-sets from the unconscious to the conscious mind. Sharpen your awareness of each mind-set that causes you to make decisions based on reaction instead of reason. Finally, ask whether adopting a certain mind-set makes you someone others would want to emulate, or not.

Define the Costs

If you have been living in denial about an ineffective mind-set—or, having become aware of one, are procrastinating about making a change—calculating the costs of keeping that mind-set is usually an extremely good motivator. What is it costing you, for instance, to put off doing your taxes until the last minute, or to slog along with an ill-trained bookkeeper rather than working with a good accountant? What is it costing you, in terms of your own physical and emotional energy at work, to delay starting an exercise program that will heighten your mind-body coordination and improve your brainpower?

Some of these costs can be measured in dollars. If that is the case, come up with a ballpark estimate. A spouse, friends, or an accountant may be able to help. Other costs are more physical or emotional, such as poor health, loss of free time, strained family relations, feelings of low self-esteem, etc. If such is the case, try to describe those states in words that will spur you to make a change. You might say something like, "My blowing up at my employees when things go wrong is counterproductive. They then feel at risk so that they start looking for other job opportunities, and I'll face a whole hiring and training challenge with new people." Match up what you consider your most ineffective mind-sets with all the "costs" you can think of, both monetary and otherwise.

Ineffective Mind-Set	Cost

Affirmations

When you discover an ideal mind-set for yourself, affirm it! Affirmations are *positive statements* of how you want your life to be, or, put a bit differently, what you want your life *to look like*. To frame up effective affirmations for yourself, follow these four simple guidelines:

1. Start your affirmation with "I am . . ."
2. State your affirmations in the present tense.
3. Describe the ideal state you aspire to achieve or project in positive terms (that is, say what you want, not what you don't want).
4. Add strong feelings.

Here are some sample affirmations:

- For the procrastinator: I am on top of things and I follow up on projects with energy and with attention to detail.
- For those who are down on themselves: I am a good and worthwhile person and others appreciate my services.
- For a person who is too withdrawn during meetings: I have good ideas and I speak them out with clarity and force as often as I can.

Remember: All mind-sets are only partially true. If you characterize yourself simply as "disorganized," you are not speaking the whole truth. Nobody is *totally* disorganized. Perhaps you are somewhat disorganized in that you lose track of papers in your office or you misfile things. But you are organized enough to keep your calendar straight and show up for all your appointments, so you are disorganized in one realm but well organized in another. Say: "I am a well-organized person. I keep my planner straight and am punctual for meetings. I can extend my good organization to other areas, and I am doing so!"

Visualization

We might describe visualization as an affirmation you can see. Instead of words, this time you affirm an ideal state of affairs with a mental image, a picture that you may see in your mind as either a snapshot or a movie. Mental images tend to evoke change in even more dramatic fashion than do words. Many world-class artists, musicians, and athletes use visualization. Golf great Jack Nicklaus, for example, runs a mental picture of his swing. He even visualizes the arc of the ball leaving the tee and soaring over the fairway, to land in a spot ideal for his second shot. Any number of pro and college basketball stars rely on visualization to "see" the ball dropping through the net long before it leaves their hands. Visualization only supports the skills learned through practice—it doesn't take the place of practice.

In a business setting you can use visualization to see employees working busily around a work hub—even before you have hired your first staffer. You can visualize a successful sales presentation, or the acquisition of a commercial building where you will be a landlord instead of a renter. The list is endless.

MODELING PEOPLE WHO HAVE "MADE IT"

Interview someone who has already achieved success in your field. (Be wary of the pure "business success"—someone may have ten million dollars in the bank and a marriage that's in pieces, or have employees who cower in fear every time he walks into the office.) How does this person see success, in business and in life? What are this person's perspectives? What are his or her mental maps? Strategies? In other words, what makes them tick?

Here are some of my favorite interview questions:

- How did you get started?
- Who mentored you (or helped you learn)?
- What did you learn?
- What strategies did your mentor(s) use to bring you along?
- How did you build on what you learned from others?
- What was your biggest mistake? Regret?

Once you discover the secrets or strategies of successful people, adopt those of their mind-sets you think will favor your personal and professional development. Do this by calling on the models we've already reviewed, including affirmations and visualization.

MIND-SETS FOR ENTREPRENEURS

One important reality of mental models is that the models that may have been very helpful to us as employees are often counterproductive for us in developing a business. Once we are building our own business, all too often we try hard to manage our lives in much the same way we did when we were a salaried employee. One commentator on business practices said, "That's like trying to drive a car from the passenger's seat."

A common mind-set of corporate employees is that it's good to be a highly trained specialist. Most corporate cultures push their people to specialize more and more as the company grows. Many times such prodding is not verbalized but is implicit in a system of encouragements and rewards. While this approach, or mind-set, suits the corporate matrix, it usually ends up being a disaster for an entrepreneur. Entrepreneurs need to develop the mind-sets of generalists. That is, it is highly desirable to know at least a bit about every aspect of your venture, from accounting to marketing to equipment maintenance.

Persistence and Patience

More than in any other area covered in this book, persistence is critical for changing mental models. Old models, ineffective in today's world of work, were wired into your brain through constant repetition from childhood. That may mean 25, 30, or 40 years of reinforcement. You have been collecting evidence for those same years, 50 to 100 thousand times, to bolster those beliefs. Do you think you can change something like that with only 20 or 50 repetitions? Unlikely. Rewiring your brain for new, more rewarding models may not be easy or quick, but it will be productive. If you don't make the effort to modernize your mind-sets, you are probably dooming your venture to weak performance—or even failure.

At this point, you have learned to be aware of everything going on around you, focus your attention, and identify and change your mind-sets. In Step 4, you'll learn how your feelings can affect the health of your business and your business relationships.

TEST YOUR INNER GAME EQ: MIND-SET

Rate yourself from 1 (weak) to 5 (strong) on how much each statement reflects your current state. Go with the first answer that comes to mind as you read each statement. Circle the number that best represents your capacity in each quiz item.

1. I am aware of having mind-sets.   1 2 3 4 5

2. I notice the effects of my mind-sets.   1 2 3 4 5

3. I see the evidence that I collect
   to prove them.   1 2 3 4 5

4. I believe I can change my mind-sets.   1 2 3 4 5

5. I am working to change my
   mind-sets.   1 2 3 4 5

Mind-set total _____

Understand the Influence of Feelings on Business

> Emotion is the chief source of all becoming-consciousness. There can be no transformation of darkness into light or of apathy into movement without emotion.
> —Carl Jung

In the old-style, or traditional, business mode, left-brain numbers crunchers led the charge—toward growth, profits, or blasting the competition. Anyone who tried to use a feelings approach to solving workplace problems was usually seen as a second-class citizen. The common work culture perception was: Feelings belong at home; here we just want to talk business.

Today, the science of management psychology has helped change that belief. Many experts now believe that there are distinct advantages to acknowledging and responding to our own feelings and those of our partners, employees, and customers.

Expressing feelings was long taboo in the workplace, probably because that arena was so dominated by men, and "real men" were not supposed to cry (or get sad or overemote or do anything else to suggest that they might be anything more than walking analytical brains). While we all inherit the ancient limbic brain, common to all primates, that gives rise to the irrational (but practical) flight-or-fight response to danger, human beings—especially men—believe we must be masters of our emotions. This mastery means never letting fear get the best of us. We tell ourselves to stay rational, or stay in control, and everything will turn out all right.

And we have often been living in denial. There truly can be things on the horizon that threaten the stability or even the survival of the enterprise we head. Falling back on such macho maxims as "grin and bear it," "just tough it out," and "when the going gets tough, the tough get going" may not always be the best mental or emotional approach, according to many who study workplace attitudes and habits.

FEELINGS ARE THE LANGUAGE OF RELATIONSHIPS

Feelings are the body's way of "talking" to you about what is going on in the environment *right now*. By effectively acknowledging these sensations and reactions, you have access to a great deal of useful information about what is going on inside of you—information that would not be provided by your thoughts alone.

The word *emotion* derives from the Latin *movere*, meaning "to move." Feelings, thus, are a form of energy—energy meant to move you in one direction or another. And this energy can and should be productively harnessed for your business decisions and dealings.

Without feelings, you would be more like a robot—able to think, but not really alive. Feelings give you your sense of aliveness, of moving through a palette of colors as you paint the activities of your day as gray or red or blue or bright yellow. Feelings can plunge you into the doldrums of regret, sorrow, or even despair; feelings can lift you to the heights of joy, exhilaration, and wonderment. In between is an incredible range of important emotional experiences such as feelings of accomplishment, satisfaction, relief, or freedom from care.

Feelings are benchmarks as you navigate the paths of your relationships, at home or at work. Relationships, in other words, shape the feelings generated in the course of those relationships. The nature and the eventual productivity of a given relationship is, consequently, determined by the way the parties feel when they interact.

WHY YOUR FEELINGS ARE IMPORTANT IN BUSINESS

Your skill with identifying, experiencing, and expressing emotions helps build relationships, and relationships are at the heart of building a business. In his book *Emotional Intelligence,* New York Times science writer Daniel Goleman lists five "feelings" skills that he says contribute greatly to your success, at home or at work:

1. Know your emotions.
2. Manage your emotions.
3. Motivate yourself.
4. Recognize emotions in others.
5. Handle relationships well.

How well you do or do not do these things will give you your emotional intelligence score, which some experts now say is a much better predictor of success than our traditional standby, intelligence quotient. While not much can be done to improve your intelligence quotient, the same is not true of your emotional quotient. With proper awareness, attention, focusing, and effort, you can raise your emotional quotient score significantly.

Communications experts tell us that only 15 to 20 percent of spoken communication is conveyed strictly by the meanings of the words a speaker uses. The rest of the meaning (and often the deepest meaning) comes through in such things as tone of voice, pauses, gestures, posture, and facial expressions.

YOUR EMPLOYEES JUDGE THEIR WORK BY HOW IT MAKES THEM FEEL

Listen when people talk about their work. They express a *feeling*. Happy employees will say: I just *love* my job. I really *enjoy* the people I work with—they're so *warm* and helpful. And my boss is really great about creating a *relaxed* atmosphere. If you goof up, you just admit it, and people will help you fix it, and then you go on.

Unhappy employees will say: I really *hate* my job. The work would be all right, but we're in such a rigid atmosphere you can hardly leave your desk without asking permission. Everybody is so *tense,* too. And the least little screwup gets blown all out of proportion. I'm always so *glad* to get out of there every evening.

Feeling appreciated is important to people. Recently, a U.S. Labor Department study reported that 46 percent of all people who quit their jobs did so because they felt unappreciated. "Felt" is the key word here.

Most of what people say they want from their jobs—or from their own venture—comes down to some form of feeling. A recent U.S. Chamber of Commerce study asked both managers and employees what the employees wanted from their work. Employees' first three desires were ranked: "feeling appreciated," "feeling in on things," and receiving help with personal problems. Spotlighting workplace disjointedness, managers rated these employee desires as numbers 8, 10, and 9, respectively.

Too often employers and supervisors overfocus on pay, ignoring the intangibles. The greatest advantage of intangible benefits is that they usually cost little or nothing. How much does it cost you to smile at your team members and say, "I'm glad you're here. I think you're doing a great job!"? How much does it cost to ask your people now and then, "How's it going? Can I do anything to help you understand your role here better or get things done?"

Good Feelings Raise Productivity

When people feel cared about and supported, they will do their utmost to live up to the trust of those who support them. This applies to your employees, potential customers, current customers, and all your suppliers.

Leadership development guru Stephen Covey explains this phenomenon using the analogy of a bank account for trust. Like a financial bank account, you make deposits. Then the quantity in the account is available for withdrawal when you need it. In other words, treat people right all the time, then when you make a mistake that has a costly effect on someone, that person will be likely to forgive you. You've reached into your emotional bank account, and found that there was a substantial reservoir of trust available. Now you can withdraw it in the form of goodwill from the person to whom you have caused some kind of trouble. Because there's mutual goodwill and trust, that person can concentrate on productivity instead of using energy to be angry or to build walls to keep you at bay.

Building this reserve of trust among people you deal with every day can make a tremendous difference in your degree of success in your venture. You can take that to the bank!

On the other hand, most people, when they feel frustrated, angry, or afraid, tend to produce less. Trying to suppress or wish away these strong feelings only makes them grow stronger. One management consultant put it this way: Stress makes people stupid. When people are emotionally upset, they cannot remember, attend to something, learn, or make decisions clearly.

Imagine the consequences of a working group when someone is unable to keep from exploding in anger or has no sensitivity about what people around him or her are feeling. On the other hand there are positive outcomes for the whole workplace when people are sensitive to others' feelings, can handle disagreements so they don't escalate into shouting matches, don't waste time and energy retaliating for real or imagined wrongs, and have the ability to promote a healthy flow of work from everyone around them.

Feelings Awareness Aids Conflict Resolution

Effective conflict resolution skills are a great boon to the entrepreneur. Most conflicts are based on feelings of anger, frustration, distrust, jealousy, fear, or resentment. Ignoring the feeling component of conflicts will reduce your effectiveness in working out a resolution. Avoiding interactions with people you consider difficult (who probably feel the same about you) makes matters worse.

In the booklet "A Model for Nonviolent Communication," Marshall B. Rosenberg, Ph.D., describes his model for conflict resolution called "Compassionate Communication," or "Nonviolent Communication."

This model requires answering these four questions:

1. What are you observing?
2. What are you feeling?
3. What are your unmet needs?
4. How can you frame a request to meet your needs?

The first question may be harder than you might imagine. As you already discovered in Step 1, Awareness, it can be difficult to separate your observations from your interpretations of a given event.

Rosenberg puts it this way:

I can handle your telling me
what I did or didn't do.
And I can handle your interpretations
but please don't mix the two.
If you want to confuse any issue
I can tell you how to do it:
Mix together what I do
with how you react to it.

Whenever you launch into attributing motives to someone or calling them names, you have stopped observing and started interpreting. So don't do it!

You can, consequently, greatly increase your personal productivity if you can learn to experience and express—in appropriate ways—your feelings and emotions. The truth is you are not fully human until you give yourself permission to express your feelings—and let others do the same in your presence.

If you manage to pinpoint and express your feelings appropriately in a given situation, you will be able to move on to answering the third question in Rosenberg's model: What are your unmet needs? Feelings will point the way to such needs—*always!*

The first step toward being happy and productive is to ask for what you need or want (at work or elsewhere). While this may seem obvious, it is not easy for everyone to do. Many people just do not, or cannot, say what they actually want. (People who do not get what they want become unhappy and, consequently, less productive.)

In pinpointing what you need or want, you are ready to take the final step in the process of conflict resolution: make a request. If you haven't answered the first three questions, you cannot even ask the fourth, much less answer it. Do you, like many people, expect people around you to read your mind and simply deliver what you need without your ever asking or explaining to them what it is? This is unrealistic. To get your needs accommodated, you must develop the habit of identifying those needs and then put them into the form of a concrete, specific request for action.

The more specific the request, the better. When possible, frame the request in a positive form. For instance, say to your partner, "Please include me in all major decision making," instead of, "Stop making decisions without consulting me." The first sentence will be better received and will increase your chances of having your partner actually behave in the manner you desire. It is amazing how willing most people will be to help us, or meet us halfway, when we phrase our requests constructively. It is equally amazing how people will dig in and resist us when we demand things in an aggressive or accusing tone.

IMPROVE YOUR EMOTIONAL INTELLIGENCE

Everyone has ideas or mind-sets about feelings, and where they do or don't belong in the workplace. Whatever you currently believe is either a help or a hindrance to experiencing, expressing, and managing feelings—your own and others'. Doing these three things will greatly improve your chances for success in your business life.

So let's pause a moment and do a short exercise. Make a list of your thoughts about feelings—positive and negative, and about what are or are not appropriate ways of expressing them. Don't edit your thoughts, just write down everything that comes to mind.

My beliefs about feelings:

_____
_____
_____
_____
_____
_____

Now, review your list. What seems to be the overall tone? Can you express that tone in a word or two? Do you seem to have a positive or a negative appreciation of feelings? What appears to be your attitude about expressing feelings at work? From whom did you learn these models? Are there any models that may have served you well when you were a child, but now are outdated?

As you read your list, you will discover how you handle feelings—your own and others'. Do you express yours or rein them in? Or does it depend on which feeling(s)? Are you OK with employees, customers, and suppliers expressing their feelings? Or does it depend on which feeling(s)? Do you try to control others' expressions of feelings? Are you successful? How much time and energy does the effort take?

To develop a workplace where feelings are never or rarely expressed, discussed, or brought into your planning, is like taking the thermostat off the wall because you don't like the temperature it is displaying. Feelings are *there* and have impact, whether you discuss them or not.

As you proceed through the rest of this chapter, consider ways you can productively use feelings, expressions of those feelings, and reflections on feelings in the course of your working day.

Be Aware of Your Feelings

If being keenly aware of your own feelings is so important, how do you get there—especially if you were not encouraged to develop this skill as a child? Most discovery will occur through asking questions of yourself and truly reflecting on the answers. Ask yourself, "What am I feeling right now? Am I feeling engaged by this subject? Fearful? Bored?" Don't judge these feelings, just notice what you are feeling and write it down.

Right now I am feeling _____
_____

If it seems somewhat strange or funny going through this exercise, take heart. You have plenty of company. According to researchers, an astonishing number of people give only the vaguest description of their feelings because they were never taught to describe those feelings even to themselves—much less someone else. Like any skill, however, it can be learned.

Your Feelings Provide a Feedback System

Feelings tell you how you are responding to your environment. You may even think of feelings as feeding information back to your body, mind, spirit, and your life in general. Are you too *cold?* Then perhaps you are not letting your real feelings register much. You may be suppressing them, in fact. Are you too *hot?* Then, on the other extreme, you may be letting your feelings run away with you—or putting your physical systems into overdrive. In a well-regulated human being, the thermostat will register the feelings and the body and mind will adjust to properly *manage* those feeling (without denying or suppressing them).

Measure the Intensity of Your Feelings

Measuring feelings, on a scale of 1 to 10 will help you quantify their intensity. You may at first think that what you are feeling is boiling rage, but if you recall another moment when you were on the brink of exploding right through the top of your head, you may decide that, no, this anger's not a 10, maybe an 8, or maybe only a 7. It helps to do this. The same goes with other emotions. A scale is especially good with something like "confusion." Just how confused are you, really? When I am flustered because I have lost something, it helps to take a deep breath and tell myself, "Either I'm going to find this item or I'm not, but staying in such a state of being upset isn't going to help me find anything." Then I can reduce my feeling of being flustered from maybe a 7 to a 4 or a 3. And if I can actually tell myself, "Good. You're calmer. Now you're in better shape to conduct a search," things usually go even better.

Identifying your feelings is good feedback, but identifying the intensity of your feelings can be equally important. Identifying feelings, listening to feedback, and measuring their intensity, all raise your emotional quotient.

EXPRESS YOUR FEELINGS

Now that you know what you are feeling, what is the best way to express your feelings? Many of us have to get over a lesson we were taught as children: It is bad to tell others how you really feel about something. Expressing feelings will hurt people; it's better just to "keep a stiff upper lip."

Think of all the other expressions current in American parlance that reinforce this tack: Grin and bear it. Don't get bent out of shape. Don't take things so hard. Lighten up. No fear. If this is your mind-set, you have a lot to overcome.

There are, however, inappropriate or counterproductive ways of expressing your feelings. For instance, telling someone, "You drive me crazy with the way you handle your projects," or "You're the cause of all my headaches because of your lack of savvy when handling customer complaints," or something similar, is to refuse to take responsibility for the way you feel, and place total blame on someone or something outside yourself. To say that others *make* you feel some way or other is to deny that you have any power over your own feelings or your own circumstances. Taking responsibility for your feelings may not be easy, but it is important. Once you have done this, you can express yourself effectively. For example, there's a world of difference between telling an employee, "You drive me crazy with your sloppy files and the way you work with papers scattered all over your desk," and telling that same employee, "When I see files out of order and what looks to me like a big mess on someone's desk, I feel panicky. I like order, and it just seems to me it must be hard to get things done right when a person doesn't keep everything neat."

Frequently, as the above example illustrates, you have to use more words to convey your sentiments when you take responsibility for your feelings and strive to avoid dumping blame on others. This will at first seem unnatural, and a waste of words. Well, it can become natural to you, with practice, and the extra words are worth it for the huge rewards you will reap in your relations with a partner, your staff, your customers or clients, and your suppliers.

What is the best way to express feelings? Just start out with "I feel" and name the emotion. If it is relevant, describe the situation. "I feel excited over getting this contract." "I feel worried that we might not be able to meet the deadline." "I feel anxious about integrating this new person into our staff." "I feel angry because nobody discussed the issues with me before making a decision."

Do not say, "I feel that. . . ." What follows, typically, is not a feeling at all, but a thought or an idea for a course of action. People of course do this all the time. ("I feel that we should go to lunch at 1 instead of at 12," "I feel that she's not treating me right," etc.) If you are among them, vow to yourself right now that you will make a change. Say, instead: "I think we should go over the plans once more before our presentation to the client." "I believe we've talked things over enough, and it's now time to come to a decision." This will put words such as "think" and "believe" in their rightful place in your communication style. It also will reserve the expression "I feel" for where it belongs: telling others how you *feel* about yourself, others, or a situation.

Remember that your expression of feelings is subjective. What you mean when you say "afraid" may be taken as more or less fearful by someone listening to you, depending on that person's own subjective use of the same word. To get more specific with your listeners, you can add degrees. "I am somewhat afraid," or "very afraid," or "terribly afraid." Another system is to go with the 10-point scale. "This fear is about a 7." Using degrees or the scale will give your listeners a much more specific notion of what your fear is like. (Or your anger or your excitement or your regret or whatever.)

Expressing Feelings Ineffectively

Here are some typical ineffective ways of expressing feelings, paired with ways that are more likely to achieve the communication results the speaker desires.

Example 1. Attributing your feelings to someone else's conduct.

You make me so mad I could spit nails.

Better:

I feel angry when you forget to mail out invoices.

When you drive 15 miles over the limit, you scare the daylights out of me.

Better:

I feel afraid when someone drives much faster than I would.

▪▪▪▪▪

Example 2. Misusing the verb "feel" to express what is not a feeling, but rather a thought, a judgment, or a belief.

I feel that you are wasting time.

Better:

It seems to me you are wasting time.

―――――――

I feel you are doing a good job.

Better:

I think you're doing a good job.

Example 3. Using words that are too vague or general to express your feelings.

I feel good.

Better:

I feel content (or jubilant or satisfied or peaceful or . . .)

I feel bad.

Better:

I feel sad (or queasy or melancholy or depressed or . . .)

Example 4. Mixing feelings and interpretations.

I'm offended by your last comment.

Better:

I feel upset when I hear someone tearing down someone else behind their back.

EXPAND YOUR FEELINGS VOCABULARY

Too often we limit our expressions of feeling to a handful of adjectives: good, bad, so-so, fine, worried, OK, down, angry, etc. We can do better.

Psychologist Rollo May, in his book *Man's Search for Himself,* had this note on the subject of expanding your feelings vocabulary: "One has a heightened sense of aliveness. Then, instead of one's feelings being limited like the notes in a bugle call, the mature person becomes able to differentiate feelings into as many nuances, strong and passionate experiences, or delicate and sensitive ones, as in the different passages of music in a symphony."

Here are some suggestions:

- Affectionate
- Afraid
- Aggravated
- Amazed
- Angry
- Annoyed
- Anxious
- Appreciated
- Bewildered
- Bored
- Calm
- Cheerful
- Concerned
- Confident
- Confused
- Curious
- Delighted
- Depressed
- Disappointed
- Discouraged
- Distressed
- Eager
- Embarrassed
- Encouraged
- Enthusiastic
- Envious
- Excited
- Fascinated
- Frightened
- Frustrated
- Glad
- Grateful
- Hostile
- Hurt
- Impatient
- Interested
- Irritated
- Lonely

- Loving
- Mad
- Nervous
- Optimistic
- Overjoyed
- Overwhelmed
- Pained
- Peaceful
- Perplexed
- Proud
- Regretful
- Relieved
- Resentful
- Sad

- Satisfied
- Scared
- Secure
- Sensitive
- Shocked
- Sorry
- Surprised
- Thankful
- Troubled
- Trusting
- Uncomfortable
- Uptight
- Worried

Some words people use to express feelings are really expressions of a feeling and an interpretation combined. These are not pure feeling words, and may cloud your meaning. Some "interpretive feeling" words are:

- Abandoned
- Accepted
- Attacked
- Belittled
- Betrayed
- Blamed
- Cheated
- Criticized
- Disliked
- Distrusted
- Ignored
- Inadequate
- Intimidated

- Misunderstood
- Neglected
- Patronized
- Rejected
- Threatened
- Unaccepted
- Unappreciated
- Unimportant
- Unloved
- Unworthy
- Used
- Victimized

Especially avoid words that have a manipulative nature to them, designed to provoke negative feelings in others (blaming, guilt, etc.). Some such words are:

- Ashamed
- Guilty
- Stupid
- Worthless
- Wrong

While it probably will be hard for you to avoid using interpretive words entirely, try to limit your use of them, using pure feeling words whenever you can. And when you hear yourself using a word in the "interpretive feeling" vocabulary category, be aware that you are mixing feeling and interpretation.

MANAGE YOUR FEELINGS

Understanding what you are feeling is one thing, managing your feelings well is another. The reason most businesses do not encourage expression of feelings is the stereotypical notion that "feelings get in the way." This can indeed be the case if people are not managing their feelings very well, and are expressing them in a destructive fashion. That is to say, in too many instances feelings get used as fuel in "the blame game." People hold grudges, talk about coworkers behind their backs, and undermine morale. That is not what I mean by "managing feelings."

To manage your feelings well, you must know: (1) what those feelings are, as specifically as possible, (2) how intensely you hold them, and (3) how best to express them so that others will take your expression as useful information, rather than as a sledgehammer attack.

Everything we have gone over thus far should help, especially the caveats about using the right word; and indicating intensity by using adverbs such as "a little," "rather," or "very"; or by points on a 1–10 scale.

You can also manage your feelings by redirecting them, as the next three sections will show.

Redirecting Feelings

Sometimes we try to manage feelings by suppressing them. There is much more public support for suppressing feelings—especially strong negative feelings—than for "blasting people out of the water" by turning an expression of feelings into something combative. Yet suppressing feelings is bad for you, and can, in subtle ways, poison the atmosphere in your workplace. Like a time bomb, suppressed negative feelings are stored up as energy, or a force field. That energy might be released as carping, nitpicking, hostile glances, various forms of "the silent treatment," grudgingness—or, if it all explodes, as one catastrophic unleashing of anger in a blow-up at one or another of the people with whom you work.

Holding in (or suppressing) your anger also has disastrous consequences for your own health. Among ill effects doctors and researchers have cited are: overeating, increased use of nicotine or drugs, high cholesterol levels, rising blood pressure, hypertension, heart attacks and other cardiovascular problems, immune system disorders, breast cancer, and greater susceptibility to such things as headaches, stomachaches, and backaches.

How do you avoid these negative consequences? You redirect your expressions of feelings to gain a positive outcome. Reread the previous sections to help you choose the right words, avoid the blame game, and still effect the changes you want.

Managing Anger

To manage anger, you must first understand where it comes from. Underneath most angry feelings lies frustration in not getting your needs or wants met. John Lee, in his book *Facing the Fire: Experiencing and Expressing Anger Appropriately,* capsules the reality of anger like this: "Anger is caused by frustration over the fact that the world is not made to satisfy our desires. Anger is thus inescapable. . . . [It is] with us in the cradle and with us as we face our death. If we are human, we get angry. Even Jesus and Ghandi got angry."

Still deeper under the frustration lies hurt. Often it is difficult to get under the anger and the frustration to the bedrock level of personal hurt. But to become aware that hurt is there, buried deep, is a good first step. Sometimes it will take a while to get beneath the surface to where the hurt simmers. Be persistent. It is of great benefit to delve beneath the anger to the level of the hurt, because then the anger will begin to dissolve and you will have only the hurt left to deal with.

A boss who typically explodes at his or her employees is angry because they are not, somehow, matching up to the boss's expectation of how, or in what time frame, a piece of work will get done. Very likely that boss has a parent (maybe even both parents) who constantly laid down tough expectations for their children, and blew up when those expectations were not met. In other words, underneath the boss's anger and frustration over staff not meeting his or her expectations is hurt from the memory of being pressured and verbally abused as a child.

Aristotle spoke of the challenge of expressing anger appropriately. "Anyone can become angry," he said. "That is easy. But to be angry with the right person, to the right degree, at the right time, for the right purpose, and in the right way . . . that is *not* easy."

To manage your anger, instead of letting it rule you, try these exercises:

- Breathe deeply for four or five minutes.
- Write down your feelings, and the circumstances that triggered the anger, in a journal.
- Vent with a caring friend (ideally, not someone involved in bringing up your anger).

Sometimes, if your anger is much larger, you may need to do some physical releasing exercise, such as kicking a soccer ball against a wall, punching a bag or pillow, or jogging.

When you can act, instead of react, you are managing your anger.

Managing Fear

Fear, like anger, is a primal emotion that seems to plague many people. Some of the forms that fear takes are: anxiety, nervousness, worry, and panic. Unlike anger, fear often is kept bottled up inside—not expressed very demonstrably by behavior immediately apparent to others.

To manage fear, you must first notice when you feel afraid. Because many people in our culture have been socialized to ignore or suppress their fears, this may take some work. (From the time you were small, how often have you heard someone older say "don't be afraid"? Thus you have learned that it is wrong to express fear.)

Underlying most fear is the thought that you will not be able to handle what you think may happen (having others discover your mistakes, being told to "shut up" if you voice a complaint or objection, or being regarded as incompetent if you require further explanations of a project).

Extreme cases of fear include paranoia or panic attacks. These waves of emotion can be so immobilizing that some people are afraid to leave their homes.

To overcome fear it helps tremendously to become deeply aware of your *self-talk*. Listen to what you are telling yourself. When we are afraid, there is always—this is 100 percent predictable—a stream of fearful thoughts running through our head. Step back from these thoughts and observe them, as if you were watching a raging river from the safety of a riverbank—not from thrashing about in the roiling waters. How likely is it that the worst-case scenario will actually happen? Even if it does, is it really something you can't survive? The answers are usually "slight" and "no." Reality is rarely as bad as our nightmares.

PILING UP REMEMBERED FEELINGS

If we were only dealing with one feeling at a time, relating to something happening in the present, things would be tough enough. What often occurs is that a present circumstance evokes a recollection of something that happened to us in the past, stirring up all the feelings we associate with that event. What a witch's brew of emotions! If we return to self-talk to bring us back to the here-and-now, we'll find the problem is much smaller and can be handled. Don't let your piled up feelings overwhelm you.

BE AWARE OF OTHERS' FEELINGS

Understanding this process is already the beginning of abating the storms that rage inside. Try to sort out the elements from the past and the present and tell yourself that what you need to do *now* is deal with the present. You may know at least one person who seems to be totally oblivious to the feelings of others. Such a person is usually not a good team player at work and not someone that others trust.

You can increase your awareness of others' feelings by becoming a better listener and empathizing with others. In so doing, you will find that the atmosphere in your workplace will improve markedly. Trust, loyalty, mutual support, and true team spirit all grow from a deepening of just this kind of emotional sensitivity.

Awareness of others' feelings leads to a heightened capacity for helping others to manage their feelings appropriately. This does not mean always giving in to or coddling those around you. It means that you may be able to allow them to vent some of their anger without you reacting to it, within reasonable boundaries. The emotional boundaries of your workplace should be broad enough to provide a space for the expression of a healthy range of feelings, but narrow enough for everyone to feel "safe."

Once you are in touch with your own feelings, you are equipped to be more sensitive to the feelings of those with whom you work. This extension of your feeling self is called empathy. To empathize with others is to notice the circumstances in which they are operating, how they are being affected by people and situations around them, and to let them know you have some understanding of their state and that you care about them.

Once you are aware of the feelings of those around you, you can begin to manage your own emotional reactions to others' feelings much better. Managing your responses will help tone down the anger, fears, and other emotional responses rising up from your employees, customers or clients, and others. Often just listening well for a protracted period, without interruptions or commentary from you, will help calm things down. And when everyone is calmer, a reasonable examination of differences, and ways to close the distance between your positions, can begin. Listening and empathizing will improve teamwork and reduce tensions in your workplace. And, as we discussed earlier, happier workers are more productive workers.

Now that you understand awareness, attention, mindsets, and feelings, you can explore how desire will light your entrepreneurial fire.

TEST YOUR INNER GAME EQ: FEELINGS

■■■■■

Rate yourself from 1 (weak) to 5 (strong) on how much each statement reflects your current state. Go with the first answer that comes to mind as you read each statement. Circle the number that best represents your capacity in each quiz item.

1. I am aware of having feelings.   1 2 3 4 5
2. I notice my feelings as I have them.   1 2 3 4 5
3. I can communicate my feelings.   1 2 3 4 5
4. I take responsibility for my feelings. 1 2 3 4 5
5. I am working to manage my feelings.   1 2 3 4 5

■■■■■

Feelings total _____

Light Your Entrepreneurial Fire

We are such stuff as dreams are made of.
—Shakespeare
The Tempest, IV:2

Desire creates: it makes something out of nothing; it is the start of all great ventures, and the fuel that propels them to high achievement. Desire undergirds the late-night planning sessions and the big-push workdays. The desire to accomplish is what lights the entrepreneurial fire.

Desire is the one quality that most entrepreneurs seem to have in abundance. One person's desire might be to succeed in dollars and cents, to be able to send children to good colleges or to retire in style. Another might be seized by the passion of an idea that seemed right for the time. Another by the drive to create a product or service that would make the world a better (or safer or friendlier) place.

You might call desire drive or passion or self-motivation or enthusiasm. Whichever term you use, you probably have a gut feeling that that quality is what gives you the energy to struggle for success. And you also realize, intuitively, that when that quality loses its punch, you start to feel like you are pushing a wheelbarrow full of rocks uphill.

Desire is contagious. The team spirit that wins contests on the gridiron or the basketball court typically develops from the aware and enthusiastic leadership of a coach and the team captains. The same is true in business. Entrepreneurs and their top employees are responsible for generating high motivation for the whole enterprise. If they *can't*—or *won't*—do it, who will?

Powerful teams form around a leader who comes to work exuding enthusiasm for the venture, and who, by verbal cues, gestures, and facial expressions, sends out signals that "It's great to be doing what we're doing!" "This is worthwhile." "We're making real progress and we're on our way!"

You can lack other qualities, such as organization, vision, and top-flight communication skills, and still get off the ground if your desire is strong enough. If you have very low desire, however, the first adverse wind of trouble will probably wipe you out.

Other skills can be delegated. If you are terrible at filing, recordkeeping, and office management, a good secretary can step into the breach. If you hate dealing with financials, a CPA with energy and integrity can work wonders. If you're poor in sales, there are sales reps who can put your products or services out on the market for you. If you lack desire, however, there's nobody you can hire to make up for what is missing inside of you.

WHERE DOES DESIRE COME FROM?

What makes certain people passionate about their life and the ventures they undertake while others languish in lukewarm torpor? The truth is, no one is entirely sure. There are theories that say that desire is intrinsic within certain personalities; others surmise that desire is a product of the right combination of person/place/business/partners/employees/

customers. In my experience a combination of these two sources seems more likely.

Often, desire is a reflection of an individual's personal power. Someone who manifests a noticeable degree of personal power—magnetism, push, capacity to galvanize others into action—frequently has an ample supply of desire. Even more typically, if a person manifests little personal power, that person will also be fairly low in desire. It's sort of a chicken-and-egg thing. Whichever comes first—personal power or desire—they go together and they make things happen as a business is growing.

The ebb and flow of desire is something else that often eludes explanation. There has been much discussion of biorhythms, chemically-induced mood swings, the effects of various diets, and of course the weather. Age too plays its part. However, the impact of circumstances cannot be discounted. A new contract is energizing, the loss of a major client account is depleting. The support of family, friends, and staff also has considerable impact on desire. So may active participation in a church or in other social organizations (scouting, bridge club, softball, etc.).

Bring your awareness and your focusing capacity to bear on your desire. See how you respond to these questions:

- What is my level of desire for my venture right now? ___

- When was my desire highest? ___

> ▪▪▪▪▪
> Why was it high then? _____
> _____
>
> ▪▪▪▪▪
> What helps to stoke my desire? _____
> _____
>
> ▪▪▪▪▪
> What can I do now to put myself in touch with the best of my desire? _____
> _____
> _____
> _____

RAISE YOUR LEVEL OF DESIRE

Desires usually are not all or nothing. They are like a dimmer switch that can be turned from very low to full brightness. From one individual to another, and from one moment or project to another, desire may range from a mild inclination to do something to the burning passion that makes a person or a team work night and day to develop a product or get a presentation ready for a major client opportunity.

The good news is that you can increase your desire levels incrementally. You don't need to push yourself to jump to a 9 on the 10-point scale. For starters you can attempt to move up from a 3 to perhaps a 5 or a 6.

IS IT DESIRE, ENTHUSIASM, OR EXCITEMENT?

A close cousin of desire, enthusiasm is an inner joy that reflects, in waves of emotion, a deeper-seated and more permanent desire. Enthusiasm, in other words, bubbles up within us from the wellspring I am calling desire. Enthusiasm produces a glow on your features that tells people that you really love what you are doing and are committed to it.

Occasionally, enthusiasm might break forth in excitement. With excitement you may be prone to move quickly and talk in high-energy spurts. You blurt out "Wow! Our fourth-quarter earnings are going to be up 20 percent and next year's looking great, too!" or "Unreal! That's our third new client this month!" Excitement may ebb and flow, but at its height it renews the flame of desire, and at its low point, the steady flame of desire keeps lit the fire of excitement. Desire maps out the road, enthusiasm keeps you on it, and excitement refuels you for the journey.

DESIRES TRIGGER FEELINGS

Feelings—emotional feelings, that is—depend to a large extent on your underlying desires. Sometimes you may think that feelings start on their own. They do not. You feel something in relation to your expectations of how things should, in an ideal world, turn out.

You desire to experience beauty in your life. So when you come face to face with it, as when driving along the ocean, you see the glorious panorama of a perfect sunset, or when you meet the first conscious stare of a newborn child, or when you hear a stirring passage of Brahms, you react with deep emotion. That emotion expresses the happy conjunction you have just experienced between desire and a reality that matches up to that desire.

Even negative emotions have a relationship to desire. For instance, you desire to live in a safe environment. So when you walk through an area you consider "safe" and see a store window pierced with bullet holes, you shudder with fear. Your desire to be safe is threatened. Similarly, in business, you may be happily cruising along in your venture when, suddenly, a conglomerate sets up shop near you, providing the same service or product you offer. You are shaken with foreboding over the challenge such competition now presents. Here too your desire to feel secure is under attack.

REMEMBER YOUR MOMENTS OF BURNING DESIRE

One of the most useful exercises I can propose to you is that you find a quiet place, away from all distractions, and put yourself through a little memory quiz. Ask that storage place of happy memories in your mind to play the film clips of your "best moments." Notice what really stirred up the highest levels of passion or desire inside of you. What did those moments feel like? Focus your attention now specifically on your business life. Recall the idea stage, the planning stage, your first day in the business, the first big rush of customers or the first major contract, or a breakthrough to a higher level of volume.

These memories can be like fuel to keep your passion burning when times are tough or uncertain. If you work hard, play fair, and deliver the best product or service you can, there will be more customers, more contracts, more sales.

> Write your best memories on the lines below:
>
> _____
> _____
> _____
> _____
> _____
> _____
> _____
> _____

EXERCISE YOUR BEST VALUES

Your values are your basic core beliefs or moral mindsets. They are the foundation of how you run your life. Some examples of values would be: work hard, treat people right, be honest, don't lose your temper, give your first loyalty to God, be open with your spouse and close friends, etc.

Live your values in the way you treat your employees and customers and suppliers; they will absolutely help you maintain a high level of desire. Compromising your values is like cheating on yourself. Your self-esteem will drop, and so will your desire.

SELF-MOTIVATION IS THE KEY TO ENDURING SUCCESS

People who are self-motivated, who can call up desire and enthusiasm when they need it, are very entrepreneurial. If you have a ready reservoir of "can-do" energy, you will always have the capacity to meet the challenge of the moment.

Self-motivation is being a self-starter. It is an essential trait for any entrepreneur. Heindre Weisinger, in his book *Emotional Intelligence at Work*, says that self-motivation means "the person must be able to take on a task or job, stick with it, move ahead with it, and deal with any setbacks." That's as good a working definition of entrepreneurship as any I know.

Acknowledging your own energy and your positive points contributes greatly to your level of self-motivation. It's funny how simple this is, and how well it works: Just telling yourself, "Hey, I'm doing a good job here. I'm making progress. Things are moving, and I'm part of making it happen," will make an effective difference. Praising yourself, just like praising your employees or your coworkers, builds motivation.

SELL WITH DESIRE

Desire impacts sales more than any other area of business. If you don't have the desire to sell, you will find it difficult to get on the phone or show up in person to sell your product or service. Desire makes you feel "up."

Mary Jane is a newsletter designer and editor who has been in business for herself for five years. For the last three-and-a-half years, her venture has been sailing along rather well. She enjoys editing and writing copy and packaging it in an attractive design, and she is known for delivering her newsletters to clients on schedule and within budget.

After four years in business, Mary Jane began to dread making sales calls. She no longer felt a burning desire to go out and add clients. Luckily for her, by then her business was well established. She not only kept her early clients, she also expanded her business through word-of-mouth referrals from those clients.

Suddenly, within a six-week period, her two largest clients called to say they had decided to do their newsletters in-house. Suddenly, 40 percent of Mary Jane's business flew out the window.

Shocked into the reality that her livelihood was now threatened, Mary Jane got a grip on herself and decided she had to find a way to rebuild her business. Working with a coach, she rediscovered her original dream of working for herself, being able to arrange her own time and work from home, and her desire to produce first-rate newsletters for a variety of clients. She asked for and received letters of recommendation from previous and current clients.

She mailed marketing packets to local Chamber of Commerce members. Within nine weeks her marketing showed impressive results and Mary Jane found herself in the midst of contract negotiations for three new clients. Her resurrected desire had won the day.

WIN BATTLES THROUGH SELF-DISCIPLINE

If succeeding as an entrepreneur were easy, everyone would do it. Often what separates the true thoroughbreds like Mary Jane from the also-rans is self-discipline, a core part of self-motivation. Like other successful entrepreneurs, she stays late when she has to, goes the extra mile, bears down on a project with keen focus, and renews her effort when adversity strikes. Mary Jane exhibits self-discipline.

Discipline implies that what you are doing is something you might rather not do—or at least not right now, or perhaps not with the single-minded intensity it takes to impress clients or customers out of their socks. So, at least on occasion, self-discipline calls you to force yourself to put forth the required effort to get the result you are after.

For some people, discipline equals a loss of freedom. But freedom to do what? To fail in business? To have to get back in harness and march to someone else's drumbeat? Discipline gives birth to freedom—the freedom to earn your living doing something you have chosen to do, to be your own whipcracker, and to organize your workplace the way it suits you. Self-discipline is not a hardship, but a gift to yourself.

> Recall when you had to exercise strict self-discipline to reach a goal. Write down these memories below; they will become the trophies that remind you that you have what it takes to succeed in business.
>
> _____
> _____
> _____
> _____
> _____
> _____
> _____

BUILD THE "IT'S ALL WORTH IT!" MIND-SET

One of my favorite mind-sets to build desire is the "It's all worth it" attitude. Believe that in the end all your sacrifices, creativity, hard work, and stick-to-it-iveness will pay off. You'll be glad you went through it all. Jumping out of an airplane with a parachute and plunging into business for yourself have a lot in common! There are risks and unknowns, rewarded with the exhilaration of learning not only to survive the effort—but to thrive in it, to draw great pleasure and satisfaction from it, and to know it's all worth it.

CREATE POSITIVE FEELINGS

"What?!" some of you may be asking. "He expects me to 'create feelings'?" Yes, I do—and you can. The capacity to create, or at least positively influence, your feelings is an invaluable skill for people building a business.

Here are some approaches:

- *Eliminate negative self-talk.* Catch yourself in the midst of a naysaying session and curtail it. If you find you are grousing, complaining, poor-mouthing, or bad-mouthing (the competition, your employees, the weather, whatever), stop!

    There is nothing that will turn your feelings sour like an extended period of grousing about one thing after another. Pretty soon nothing looks very bright. It may be a splendid, sunshiny day, but because you're all caught up in straightening out accounts that are overdue, you may miss the blue skies and the smiling mood of passersby right outside your window.

- *Affirm yourself and your people.* Create only positive self-talk. Post your affirmations on the wall over your desk if you have to, but find a way to bring them to your attention on a daily basis. Here are some sample affirmations: We're heading in the right direction. We are capable of fulfilling the mission we've set for ourselves. Today is a great day to be alive. I am the maker of my moods, and I choose to be happy.
- *Do the "YES" exercise.* There is something magical about the word "yes." Just repeat it out loud to yourself two or three times right now: "yes, Yes, YES!" Better still, shout it out "YES!!!" Doesn't that feel wonderful?

  One consultant has his workshop participants repeat the word faster and faster, louder and louder, and then he builds them to a crescendo of one last loud "Y E S !" After doing this exercise it is hard to help but feel motivated, energized, and excited.
- *Visualize the successful outcome you desire.* If you are caught up in the humdrum of fighting the daily battles of business, reclaim your dream. Picture once again how your venture will look in its optimal state—a new building, a covey of happy employees, a network of satisfied accounts, continuous growth. Good visuals in your imagination will help you create a plan to reach your goals.
- *Hire a coach.* One of the big benefits of having a business coach is that he or she will support and reinforce your desires. Coaches seem to have extra doses of desire and energy themselves, and those doses are ready for and available to clients. (We'll return to coaching in Step 6 and discuss it in more detail.)
- *Recreate yourself through recreation.* The old saw about "all work and no play" is true. You can work, work, work yourself right into burnout, a heart attack, or

oblivion. Discover what you really enjoy doing for recreation, and then don't let wild horses stop you from fitting it in. Tennis, handball, volleyball, cycling, long walks in the park, or canoeing on a river or lake, go for it! The vitality and sparkle your recreation will give you will pay its own dividends during the time you spend at work.

- *Have fun on the job.* You heard it right: have fun. Some of the most successful businesses I know make having fun a major priority, and the customers and clients seem to enjoy the atmosphere that is created. A little bit of joking at work is a tonic for doing the heavy lifting or serious planning or executing the no-nonsense tasks of the day. How about a dartboard for dart breaks? A chess game moving forward at just a couple moves each per day? What would you and your employees like to do? Fun shouldn't get in the way of work, but any workplace or work schedule can make room for a little fun every day.

Now let's take a close look at your habits—especially those that may be holding you back.

TEST YOUR INNER GAME EQ: DESIRE

Rate yourself from 1 (weak) to 5 (strong) on how much each statement reflects your current state. Go with the first answer that comes to mind as you read each statement. Circle the number that best represents your capacity in each quiz item.

1. I am aware of my desire.   1 2 3 4 5

2. I notice the intensity of my desire.   1 2 3 4 5

3. I am aware of what motivates me.   1 2 3 4 5

4. Disappointment does not kill my desire.   1 2 3 4 5

5. I keep my motivation level high.   1 2 3 4 5

Desire total   _____

Build Strong Business Habits

> We are what we repeatedly do. Excellence, then, is not an act, but a habit.
> —Aristotle
> *Nicomachean Ethics*

Entrepreneurs, perhaps more than salaried workers, live or die according to whether they can capitalize on the habits that already bolster their chosen endeavor, and identify and conquer their unhelpful habits. "First we make our habits," John Dryden once wrote, "and then our habits make us."

Do you fear cold calling? How do you go about putting off such calls? How much business are you losing because you are letting fear rule your behavior?

Or perhaps you have never acquired the good habit of being able to remember people's names. When you meet them on a second or third occasion, you have to apologize and say, "Excuse me, but . . . what was your name again?" If networking provides the link that holds your business together, you have an incredibly weak link.

Maybe your primary problem is a disorganized office. Do your files look like Attila the Hun just ran his hordes through them? Have you come to believe that saving receipts and writing down travel mileage is something only trained CPAs ever do?

All these—and many more—behavior quirks relate to the habits you have developed from early childhood on. Interrupting instead of listening, clumsiness, poor time management, weak people-to-people skills—all these come under the rubric of "habits." Haven't these traits been the subject of many a New Year's Resolution? And by March or April, where are you? All too often, still stuck in the habits you vowed to change.

So how can you come to grips with unwanted habits, *really* change for the better, and keep the magic happening month after month? By recollecting the work we did on mental models in Step 3, and by adding some insights and techniques here, you'll enjoy a clearer understanding of habits and learn how to make lasting changes.

Habits are formed by repetition—not by planning and thinking. They are like an airplane running on automatic pilot. After you do something over and over a number of times, you just file that action away, and keep on doing it. Orison Swett Marden, founder of *Success* magazine, summed it all up beautifully when he said: "The beginning of a habit is like an invisible thread. Every time we repeat the act we strengthen the strand, add to it another filament, until it becomes a great cable and binds us irrevocably, *thought and act*."

The patterns associated with the habit are engraved on our brains. Like the old black-and-white movies, when the Model T's tires got into those road ruts, it was nearly impossible for them to get out. The same thing happens with behaviors etched deeply in our brain.

Most experts believe that habits are controlled by the subconscious mind. Unlike the conscious mind—that of which we are fully aware—the unconscious floats beneath the surface of our awareness. The conscious mind constitutes only a small part of what makes us say and do things; most of our mental processes are anchored in our much larger subconscious. A change in the conscious mind is like putting a bandage on a cut; but a change in the subconscious mind is like healing the cut.

SEE THE HABIT

You can't change a habit until you see yourself doing it. So the first step to getting rid of an unsupportive habit that is holding you back in your business is to heighten your awareness of it. Catch yourself in the act! Are you always stretching at meetings or keeping your hands up on your chin or tugging on your ear? You are probably vaguely aware that these things annoy other people and hence are counterproductive for selling yourself, your ideas, or your products. Fix your attention on this particular habit, maybe by having a meeting videotaped or by asking someone you know and trust to give you a signal during a meeting that says, "There you go, doing that obnoxious gesture again."

> Think of some habits that you were unaware of at some point in the past, but then suddenly or gradually became aware of. On the lines below, list these habits and, if possible, when you became aware of them.
> _____
> _____
> _____
> _____

The methods I spoke about in Step 1 for increasing awareness are all necessary for changing our habits. Concentrating your attention, as we saw in Step 2, likewise facilitates the changing of habits. The better you become at concentrating your attention, the more likely you will be to successfully trade in old habits for new ones that will march with you on the road to success, instead of dragging you back or leading you off on tangents.

FOUR CYCLES FOR ALTERING BEHAVIORS

The process of change for altering behaviors moves through four distinct stages of awareness and competence:

1. Not knowing that you are not good at something: *unconscious incompetence*
2. Knowing that you are not good at something: *conscious incompetence*
3. Consciously becoming good at something: *conscious competence*
4. Becoming able to do something without thinking about it: *unconscious competence*

Simply put, we move from not knowing that we are doing something ineffective, to knowing but doing it anyway, to trying out a new behavior that is more effective, to doing the new behavior so that it begins to feel natural and work effectively.

Think back to learning to ride a bicycle. As a small child you knew nothing about keeping your balance on a bike and propelling it forward (unconscious incompetence). Then, as you got older, you saw other children riding, and you knew you weren't able to ride a bike (conscious incompetence). So your Mom or Dad bought you a small bike and started you out with training wheels. Soon there came that special moment when they took the training wheels off and you wobbled down the lane on a bike (conscious competence). Before long, you were able to ride a bike automatically and even give your attention to other things—traffic, the scenery, or listening to music as you rode (unconscious competence).

Try to recall a time when you went through all four of these stages in your business. In other words, a time when at first you started out unaware and incompetent in some business practice or mode, then you went to knowing that you were incompetent. Next you focused your attention and changed your behavior to conscious (i.e., somewhat awkward or forced) competence, and finally you arrived at unconscious competence where the new behavior had become second nature and felt natural.

Write about your personal experience with the four stages for altering behavior:

_____
_____
_____
_____
_____
_____
_____
_____

CHANGE HABITS THE WAY YOU CHANGE MIND-SETS

There's a clear parallel between changing mind-sets (Step 3) and changing habits. Thus, we will call on most of the techniques we covered with mind-sets and add a few special methods that work remarkably well for external change, such as habits. Each technique works well enough on its own, but when you can combine two or more techniques in the change process, you get a synergistic effect with a multiplying factor—like two times two equals sixteen!

Just as mind-sets or beliefs affect all areas of your life, so do habits. A mind-set that will help in your endeavor to upgrade your habits is, "I'm getting better and better every day at changing my habits." I like this one because it doesn't make a huge jump and state outright "I am changing my habits"—it simply hints at progress. Seeing yourself doing the thing you want to change (such as not scratching your nose or cheek during a meeting), plus a little time, may be all the technique that's required for many small and highly unconscious habits.

More time, and more effort, are needed to change more pervasive habits (such as generally poor organization of an office). The "catch-yourself-in-the-act" method, however, still works. You want to regularly move your awareness closer to the act itself. At first, you will likely notice your offending act well after it has been carried out. Don't fret. This is par for the course. Keep moving your noticing closer and closer to the act. In the process you learn to concentrate your attention on the undesirable habit. One day you will notice your habit immediately after you've done the act. And then you will notice yourself as you begin to do it. The final step is to notice yourself before you do the act (as in when your hand is just beginning to rise from your lap in order to scratch your nose). This conscious noticing will finally give you the option of either doing the act, very consciously, or refraining from doing it. Small steps lead to giant strides.

PUT A PRICE ON BAD BEHAVIOR

An excellent tactic that will work for all kinds of habits involves calculating the cost of allowing the undesirable habit to continue. List very detailed and specific costs that you pay because of one or more unwanted habits. Costs might include: Procrastination = missed sales opportunities. Missed deadlines = stress. Inability to handle conflict = damaged business relationships.

List your costs on the lines below:

_____
_____
_____
_____
_____
_____

CALCULATING THE BENEFITS OF A GOOD NEW HABIT

Now list the benefits of acquiring a habit with positive effects. Be specific. Take the case I cited at the beginning of this step, the individual who shirks cold calling even though she should be out knocking on doors or phoning people to promote her financial services firm. This businesswoman could give herself a "trial-run" week and spend two entire

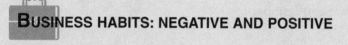

BUSINESS HABITS: NEGATIVE AND POSITIVE

Negative Business Habits

- Not checking in with current customers
- Forgetting people's names (especially customers' names)
- Putting off recordkeeping or doing a haphazard job of it
- Giving up too soon on likely prospects
- Not having goals that are clear and attainable
- Not writing your goals down and not reviewing them periodically
- Not welcoming the opportunity to solve customer complaints
- Overseeing employees' work too loosely or haphazardly
- Telling everyone that your way is the only way

- Not seeking advice from experts
- Doing marketing "only when you need to"
- Acting as if you know it all
- Operating without a business plan to guide you

Positive Business Habits

- Following up with prospects promptly and cordially
- Remembering names
- Doing recordkeeping every week
- Using a tickler file and calling customers and prospects
- Setting and updating goals
- Having an open-door policy with employees
- Acknowledging good work
- Telling employees—in private—about areas they need to work on
- Trying to hear and understand other people's perspectives
- Reviewing important issues with a coach, consultant, or mentor
- Doing marketing and sales every week
- Studying industry developments
- Reviewing and updating your business plan every six months

days making cold calls, pushing herself right through her fears and her hesitancies. The next week she could follow up all leads that sounded moderately to highly positive. She would then compare those two weeks with the lackluster business she had drummed up over preceding weeks, and also project, with an accountant, what her business could be like if she kept up the new pace as a regular practice.

Conquering a dragging-down habit like fear of cold calling could mean a new lease on life for our financial services entrepreneur. Higher volume of business, more personal income, increased satisfaction and confidence and, over time, lowered levels of stress while cold calling, are all benefits to anticipate. What a great return for changing just one habit! When you contrast the cost of hanging onto an old habit versus the benefits of trading it in on a new habit that brings your business to life, the change process looks a whole lot more inviting than it may have before.

DON'T LIE TO YOURSELF

Behind most of our habits lies a comfortable rationalization—a piece of "self-talk" that has convinced us that, "This behavior isn't so bad—lots of people do it." This lie reinforces or supports our laggardness or messiness or whatever it is. It is not as if the behavior would not still be there if the lie were removed, but the lie does make changing the habit that much harder.

Common lies linked to habits are "It doesn't matter," or "It doesn't do much harm," or "Now isn't the best time, I'll get to this later." Usually in a subconscious fashion these are the kinds of things we say to ourselves before, during, or after we practice the harmful or unwanted habit. We use this kind of self-talk to reduce our guilt and allow ourselves to avoid change. If we are convincing enough, it becomes OK to keep the habit. Uncovering the lie and bringing it out into the light of day often may provide the impetus you need to start changing a habit you really ought to ditch.

> What are the most common lies you tell yourself about your ineffective habits?
>
> _____
> _____
> _____
> _____
> _____
> _____

REWARD YOURSELF FOR MAKING A CHANGE

Using rewards to promote positive change goes back a long way. Behaviorists ever since Pavlov—remember the dogs and the bells—have used rewards to condition responses. What gets rewarded gets reinforced and gets done right, as organizational development specialists are fond of saying.

Define specific rewards to get you to change the habit that is currently your target. Select rewards in all price ranges. (Be sure to catalog rewards other than food. Especially the health-conscious among us do not want to associate change only with pampering the palate.) Great rewards might include massages, manicures, an extra game of golf, taking yourself out to a movie or on a weekend trip, or buying yourself a book or other small gift.

TRACK YOUR RESULTS

Organizational guru W. Edwards Demming said, "Anything you can track, you can manage." Track your bad habits and then track your efforts to eliminate them or substitute good habits. Tracking will give you what is often called a "key measure." A key measure (as we discussed in Step 2) is any technique that can translate into a number you can track, in case you are tracking habits or behaviors. By tracking them with numbers you can gauge how much you are focused or moving ahead on your changes.

Display your progress on a graph; it's a great way to visualize where you were, where you are, and where you are headed.

Charts and graphs give you a lot of detail at a glance. That is why Community Chests set up a huge thermometer in the public square to show rising levels of a fund-raising effort or a blood drive. Such displays powerfully convey three aspects of the effort:

1. The goal or end result
2. Where the effort is at any given moment
3. An implicit call to action or participation

The call to action is not so much spelled out as implied, but it is implied strongly. And a call to action is exactly what you need to change a habit. The display on a graph or chart of your key measures heightens your awareness and impels you toward productive change.

VISUALIZE YOUR END RESULT

Professionals in many fields—from sports to music to showbiz—mentally imagine themselves playing the perfect round of golf or playing a symphony at a world-class level—before they step up to the challenge of the first hole or a packed concert hall. This tactic works just as well in business. Your subconscious mind cannot tell the difference between the carefully imagined dress rehearsal and the real thing. Applied to, for instance, a sales call, this would mean imagining the successful navigation of all the tricky steps that such a call involves.

Make your imaging as real and as detailed as possible. Add color, 3D, texture, sounds, up-close picturing, and feelings. Always see the process unfolding from your own personal perspective. Then, as you move through the steps to change the habit, match up what is actually happening with the way you visualized it.

Now bring feelings in to play. As you see the changes taking place in your mind's eye, let your feelings speak to you of how you will feel about yourself as the new, more efficient—or more suave—you. As you learned in an earlier step, feelings and desires are your fuel to power you toward productive change. The stronger you feel the feelings, as you visualize the process, the more quickly change will occur.

DO YOU ASSOCIATE YOUR HABIT WITH PLEASURE OR PAIN?

Some of the most striking methods for changing habits are found in Anthony Robbins's material. In *Unlimited Power,* Robbins outlines ways to change any unwanted habit. He first guides you to see what you associate with your present habit, and what you associate with the more productive new habit you seek to acquire. Typically, these associations will involve either pleasure or pain. Have you sold yourself on the idea that cold calling is inherently painful? If so, you can begin to grasp why change itself can be so difficult. For you to change the aversion to cold calling, you may have to consciously decide to associate the practice with something pleasurable. If you control the images you see when you think of the habit you want to acquire—such as having a positive approach to cold calling—you'll find that making the change becomes easier and more appealing.

HIRE A COACH

Coaching is widespread in sectors far beyond sports. There are now whole schools whose aim is to train coaches—for just about everything, for academics, for music and theater, and, yes, for business, too. Coaches help develop skills that are essential to winning performance.

Coaches can be somewhat expensive—hourly rates of $50 to $150 or more—but if you make a major change through such an outlay, the cash you reap can far outweigh the cash you spend. Also, people tend to take a change process more seriously if they are spending money to facilitate it.

Here are four quick tips for hiring a coach:

1. Choose someone with whom you can feel at ease and whom you can trust.
2. Put great emphasis on the quality of the coach's listening skills. If you don't feel that what you are saying is really being received and understood, look further.
3. Hire a coach who is already self-focused. Only a focused person can help *you* get focused.
4. Finally, choose a coach who can continually focus your attention on the habit you desire to achieve. It is all too easy to get off track in the change process. A coach who gently guides you back on course is priceless.

Your coach should be able to employ any of the techniques already discussed in this step. The key measure technique, with visualization by a graph or chart, works especially well in combination with coaching.

When meeting with your coach, by phone or in person, start by examining the goals you set together during the last session. Describe what you actually did. How does reality measure up to goals? The two of you can then discuss what worked and what didn't, and how you can apply yourself to do better next time.

The added power in focusing your efforts on what you are trying to change makes hiring a good coach a worthwhile move. In the course of an entrepreneur's typically hectic day, it is easy to lose track of what habits you are trying to change. A coach won't lose track, but will be right there to focus you if you have let your resolution get lost in the shuffle of paperwork and phone contacts. Remember: One of your goals is to develop habits that will lead to your building a successful business.

LIST YOUR ACCOMPLISHMENTS—AND FEEL GRATEFUL!

> On the lines below, list all the habits you have changed throughout your entire life. (Continue on a separate paper, if necessary.) Did you learn a sport, improve your speaking style, adopt better study habits, or grow a business?
>
> _____
> _____
> _____
> _____
> _____
> _____

This list tells your self-talk that you can make changes, that you are not hopelessly stuck in procrastination, disorder, forgetfulness, etc. Review your list, feel the pride and excitement of each breakthrough, revel in the power to redesign yourself.

Be thankful for your victories and accomplishments. Generate the feeling of gratefulness for each thing on your list. Nothing supports the change process better than thankfulness, or gratitude, for progress already achieved. Such gratefulness will provide you with the added motivation to keep plugging away at change. And when change comes hard, remember your past accomplishments and feel thankful for them. This will keep you on track.

COMBINE TECHNIQUES

The techniques we've looked at thus far are good by themselves, and even more powerful in combination. Here's a little scenario that will show you what I mean:

Julia has been struggling for years with the problems of helter-skelter recordkeeping and a generally messy office. With the new coach she has hired, she calculates the costs to her operation of continuing to work in a disorganized fashion. The total time, energy, and money lost, as represented on a graph the coach has constructed, convey a clear-cut and overwhelming message: "I can't go on like this. There must be a better way."

She and her coach set goals for creating an up-to-date filing system and acquiring the software to track her financials carefully, day by day. In the course of doing this, they uncover the lie Julia had been using to keep reorganization at bay: "My girlfriend is disorganized too, and yet her business is doing OK." However, the girlfriend has a product line that is without much competition in the area and the high demand compensates for her messiness.

Julia had never had a massage before her coach suggested one as a reward. Now, for every benchmark of progress that she achieves in her quest for productive organization, she allows herself to schedule another half-hour session with her massage therapist—and she loves it!

Now that you have added the skill of building good business habits to awareness, attention, mind-sets, feelings, and entrepreneurial fire, combine them to increase your personal productivity.

TEST YOUR INNER GAME EQ: HABITS

Rate yourself from 1 (weak) to 5 (strong) on how much each statement reflects your current state. Go with the first answer that comes to mind as you read each statement. Circle the number that best represents your capacity in each quiz item.

1. I am aware of having habits.   1 2 3 4 5

2. I notice my habits.   1 2 3 4 5

3. I notice which habits are effective and which are ineffective   1 2 3 4 5

4. I observe my habits as I perform them.   1 2 3 4 5

5. I am in the process of changing my ineffective habits.   1 2 3 4 5

Habits total _____

STEP 7

Increase Your Personal Productivity

If I had eight hours to chop down a tree, I'd spend six hours sharpening an ax.
—Abraham Lincoln

Entrepreneurs need to improve on efficiently using their time and energy, and that of their people. Good news: It's all within your reach.

There are tested methods and techniques that can enhance your productivity and make better use of your working time. So why did I not simply write a book on "time management"? First, "time management" is a misnomer. You cannot manage time; you can only manage yourself—your thought processes, habits, and energy levels.

Second, to start with the techniques detailed in this step would have been like beginning to erect a building from the second floor up—minus the foundation. The first half of this book laid down a foundation of awareness and attention, and then helped you focus on your current mind-sets, feelings, and habits. This is a critical process if you are to make effective shifts in your mental and emotional approaches to your work and the way you move through your work day.

PERSONAL PRODUCTIVITY IS THE LIFEBLOOD OF YOUR VENTURE

Contrast these two scenarios: You go to work, get snafued by nonessentials (incoming telemarketing calls, searching for files missing in action, getting sidetracked at the coffee bar), and finish the day with little to show for your time. You have put in a day of low, or weak, personal productivity. On the other hand, you arrive at your desk and consult a well thought-out list of to-do assignments for the day, keep distractions to a minimum, and move through the list with crisp efficiency. Very possibly you do not manage to check off every single item on your list, but you accomplish 12 out of 14. You can count it a day of high personal productivity.

So many things to do, so little time. This is why entrepreneurs frequently bemoan the fact that a day contains only 24 hours, and they need to "waste" seven or eight of them on sleep.

Getting a solid grip on the concept of personal productivity is key to winning the battle against distractions and off-target prioritizing of what needs doing. Personal productivity, rather than time management, puts the emphasis on personal, individual input into the process and it describes results.

"Productive" can be defined as "marked by abundant production." Abundant! Don't you love the sound of that? So how do you get to the point of regularly achieving abundant production in your business? Fasten your seatbelts and let's take a ride through the process.

MAKE GIANT LEAPS IN PRODUCTIVITY

The elements below support a comprehensive system designed to increase productivity. What differentiates this list from others you've seen is its basis in awareness and attention, tying everything together in a comprehensive system.

The elements of that system are:

- Setting and revising goals
- Writing action plans
- Jotting down to-do lists for each day
- Prioritizing items on each day's list
- Noting what works well and what doesn't
- Sharpening your focus
- Fine tuning routines and schedules
- Acknowledging results

In the pages that follow we shall explore each of these components, and measure the value of each and its relationship to the overall system. This step, however, will continue beyond these points into a second set of components important for putting you and your venture solidly into the success zone. Do not skip around. This discussion proceeds sequentially, like crossing a brook from one stepping stone to the next.

GOALS: A YARDSTICK FOR PRODUCTIVITY

You need goals to measure productivity. Write them down. What you keep in your head has a way of becoming nebulous, and less than compelling as a motivating force. Writing down goals is a declaration of your commitment to them.

Productivity is measured against three levels of goals:

1. *Long-term goals.* Project these out at least five years. Say where you would like to be then and what you want your venture to look like. For instance, "We will

be a $2 million company in annual sales, with at least ten employees and an attractive headquarters of at least 2,000 square feet." Do not limit long-term goals to the financial arena. You might say, "We will be a close-knit team and have in place effective systems for taking in suggestions, resolving differences, deciding on priorities and courses of action; each person will have an opportunity for rejuvenating vacation time and profit sharing as we grow."
2. *Medium-term goals.* These goals cover the next four to five years. These goals might state a percentage of growth—8 percent, 12 percent, 25 percent, or more. Such goals might also include a plan for customer development—adding ten new clients a year, for example, for an advertising agency or a market-research firm; achieving 80 percent occupancy for a motel; or a certain volume of diners for breakfast, lunch, and dinner for a restaurant. This level might pinpoint additions to—or upgrades of—your essential equipment and tools. For instance, a new vehicle for a landscaping service, computers and software for an office operation, etc. Write detailed goals. Anticipate changes in your market, your customer base, and maybe even the focus of your business. Medium-term goals must support your long-term goals.
3. *Short-term goals.* Depending on your enterprise, these could be daily, weekly, monthly, or quarterly. Remember that your short-term goals must support both your medium-term and long-term goals.

Let's get started. Make a commitment to continuously revise your goals as you develop your business. Some you set now may turn out to be too ambitious or unrealistic; others may turn out to be too limiting or wimpy.

My long-term goals for my business are:

1. _____
_____

2. _____
_____

3. _____
_____

My medium-term goals for my business are:

1. _____
_____

2. _____
_____

3. _____
_____

4. _____
_____

5. _____
_____

My short-term goals for my business are:

1. _____
_____

■ ■ ■ ■ ■

2 _____

3 _____

4 _____

5 _____

6 _____

7 _____

8 _____

9 _____

10 _____

11 _____

12 _____

Keep a notebook of these goals so you can measure progress and update your goals.

Look over your goals now. Have you included a target date for each level? Setting target dates is key to productivity. A target date keeps you focused, on track, and constantly measuring your progress.

Definitely set goals for intangibles, such as achieving a certain level of harmony among your staff, or "flow" (as discussed in Step 2), or heightened awareness, etc. Try to link these goals to specific behaviors or actions to keep them as concrete, practical, and measurable as possible. For example, a goal for improved harmony among staff might be translated into something like having everybody keep an informal scoresheet of misunderstandings, snubbing type behavior, failure to keep everybody in the loop informed, etc. You don't want names, nor specifics, just numbers of incidents such as these per month. As the incidents lessen you'll know you are making progress toward harmony.

Action Plans: Your Practical Guide to Getting Things Done

For each goal, develop a series of steps to meet that goal. This series of steps is called an action plan. Ask yourself: I'm here, the goal's over there, what do I need to do—step by step—to get from here to there?

Here are tips on how to write your action plan:

- To quote Stephen Covey, "Start with the goal in mind."
- Make each step separate and distinct.
- Make each step measurable.
- For large goals, work backward from the goal.
- If you find yourself faltering, you have made the steps too big. So break down the big steps into smaller ones.

- Chart which items can be done simultaneously, and which need to await the accomplishment of the previous step before they can be undertaken.
- Use visual displays to help you track your progress.

WRITE TO-DO LISTS

To-do lists—done right, and followed almost religiously—are the cornerstone of a good personal productivity system. Here are some of the forms that to-do lists commonly take:

- Items written on an erasable board, posted in a highly visible location (such as just over your desk)
- Items written into a portable planner, such as Daytimer or the Franklin planner. A column is specifically reserved for today's projects and that (not in other squares, such as appointments or expenses or miscellaneous) is where the to-do list should go.
- Items logged into a pocket-sized electronic planner
- Items posted on slips of paper on a bulletin board adjacent to your desk

Different people use different systems. Whatever works really well for you is what you should stay with. You might, however, experiment with other systems just to see, for a short period, whether you can improve on what you are currently using.

Some people like to double up on their to-do lists, using multiple methods. This can be effective if you are likely to forget something simply because you are, temporarily, away from your main system. It is, however, time consuming. In most cases it is more efficient to choose one system and stay with it.

The best system for you is the one that you are comfortable with and that you use efficiently. The key to productivity is using the list well.

To use your list well, you must:

- Have the list in a conspicuous place, so that you notice it as you move through your day, and the sight of the list itself spurs you along.
- Prioritize the items on the list in order to be sure that you accomplish what is primary and not let the secondary and tertiary items gobble up all your time.
- Have some system for checking off items that you have handled. But keep the list of what you have finished so you know what you did, when you did it, and that it is accomplished.

Eugene Griessman, author of *Time Tactics of Very Successful People*, offers this advice:

> Periodically review your list. Look at it first thing in the morning, without fail. If you make sure that everything you intend to do gets on your comprehensive list—and if you check that list regularly—there is no way that anything will ever fail to be done just because you forgot about it.

Obviously, most to-do lists focus on short-term planning—the day-by-day or week-by-week kind. Remember to put the steps for reaching your long-term goals on your to-do list. Then you can see progress toward those goals. Put your medium-term and long-term goals on the wall. You won't be able to check them off so quickly, but when you do, you will truly have occasion to celebrate!

PRIORITIZE YOUR GOALS

What should you tackle first this morning? Everyone needs some system for deciding. The worst system is "whatever I feel most like doing." So set priorities.

The first principle of prioritizing is to rate items on some scale of urgency or importance. For instance:

1 = Extremely urgent
2 = Urgent
3 = Very important
4 = Important
5 = Routine

You could also either write or underline your items in different colors:

Red = Five-alarm fire (Urgent)
Orange = Important
Yellow = Needs doing
Blue = Routine

A simple system in two parts ("important" and "less important") is to circle only the important items.

(No matter what system you use, items will tend to move from "important" to "urgent" or from "routine" to "important" if you keep putting them off. Bearing down on taxes may be marked "routine" in the middle of a quarter, but by the last week of that quarter you will have had to upgrade it to "urgent.")

Know your body rhythms and your daily zones of high, low, and medium attention-focusing capacity. You, personally, may not do written work well early in the morning. So, even though writing a report may be the first priority of the day, you may do better to get other things off your desk before tackling the writing. Meetings can be tricky, as I mentioned earlier. Just after lunch is usually a bad time to hold a meeting because people are getting through the digestion process and may be sleepy. So take such things into consideration.

On a day-by-day basis, some people find they are better off doing the little things first and working into the more challenging items starting in, say, mid-morning. For others, it is just the reverse.

Finally, there is the return-on-time-invested method. Evaluate just how great a benefit you will generate by accomplishing each item—rating each perhaps on a scale of 1 to 5—for the estimated amount of time the item will consume. This will give you a figure you can compare against figures for other items on the list.

Choosing a System

Stick with your current system if it seems to be giving you good results. Changing systems is hard. However, if you believe one of these methods improves on what you are currently using, have the courage to make an adjustment. Use your inner game techniques of awareness, attention, reviewing of mind-sets and feelings, and modifying of habits to move you through the challenge of change.

Everybody is a little different from everybody else. Therefore, what works astonishingly well for one entrepreneur may give only so-so results for another. Feelings do count: Don't try to squeeze yourself into a box where you don't fit.

Note What Works Well (and What Doesn't)

Awareness! Here it will serve you very, very well. Use your awareness skills to notice what is working for you each day in terms of consulting and moving through your to-do list and actually getting things done. Notice also what isn't working so well. Ask yourself awareness questions such as:

- When am I particularly productive? Why is this so?

- How can I draw forth from within myself the energy, focusing, and other qualities I need to achieve the kind of productivity I have had in certain peak experiences?
- Are there other people who seem to facilitate my being productive? When they are not around, what can I do to behave the way I do when they are present?

> Below, answer the above personal productivity questions. (If you like, run the answers together into a little essay.)
>
> _____
> _____
> _____
> _____
> _____
> _____
> _____

Keep a written record of what works well for you and what doesn't, in your efforts to heighten personal productivity. This record draws your own map to productive change.

Sharpen Your Focus

Remember the Zen saying, "Do what you are doing while you are doing it." It applies here in a major way. Much of good personal productivity comes down to being focused on just what you are doing, moment by moment. One young CEO of a company that went from startup to $50 million in eight years, has this quality to a high degree. Should you be fortunate enough to attract his attention, he will give you 100 percent of his focused energy while you are speaking to him. He will maintain an almost dynamic eye contact with you and give you the complete assurance that what you are saying is important to him, that you are someone who is worth listening to. He may keep the conversation short as he has many other things on his agenda every day, but he will allow you to complete your message and let you know that he has received it. This is what focusing is all about.

Becoming sharply focused involves learning how to concentrate your attention intensely, on whatever you are doing. It takes practice, but is well worth your patience and effort to develop. People will notice the difference in you after you have attained this skill. You will command much more respect from partners, team members, suppliers, and clients once you have the capacity to focus sharply.

Right here would be a good time to go back to Step 2 and reread the section on "Flow" (pp. 17–19). Can you appreciate, as you read, just how much achieving this state would mean for increasing your productivity? The real trick is to be able to step into this state whenever you need it. The techniques you have learned thus far in this book relating to mind-sets, feelings, desire, and habits will all help you work toward getting into the flow whenever you need it most.

Fine-Tune Your Routines and Schedules

Routines and schedules offer structure in what often feels like a very unstructured world. They are your friends. However, there is a problem: Many small business owners got into their venture at least partly to escape from the "strait-jacket" of routine. In a word, they wanted more freedom. This is fine—up to a point. Having a business life that is too unstructured, however, is not effective for heightening productivity.

Routines will keep you on track. Scheduling things in some regular fashion—whether staff meetings or time for paperwork or for new customer prospecting—will likewise help you meet deadlines for achieving certain goals and move forward.

Here is a hypothetical routine for an independent marketing consultant:

- Monday: Client prospecting and developing, touching base with existing clients, gathering material for the newsletter.
- Tuesday–Thursday: Out-of-the-office calls on clients, on-site evaluations, conferences, coaching sessions, review of client materials such as brochures and sales letters, etc.
- Friday: Report writing, billing, and other paperwork.

A routine such as the above will give you a concrete sense of just what you have to do to make your business profitable. Once you schedule things, such as on-site client visits, you are virtually forced into doing the work that you need to do to earn your living.

Setting deadlines for yourself—and locking them in with promises to clients or customers or staff—is another way of generating productive energy.

Internal deadlines are those you set by simply scheduling yourself and/or your people to finish something by a given date. Although clients or customers are not brought in on these deadlines, meeting them is necessary to create the steps that lead to achieving medium- and long-term goals.

Both internal and external deadlines are good for business. A business that tries to run without any deadlines is often a business that is in danger of being simply dead.

Acknowledge Results

Isn't it wonderful to check off one to-do item after another—especially if an item is on the order of "renew major contract"! Finishing projects and physically checking them off as done is energizing in itself. You will feel more drained and worn out on days when you leave many things unfinished than on days when, though you may have worked like a drayhorse, your to-do list has been whittled down to few or none to go. As the act of completing things actually generates energy, why not use it often?

ONWARD TO THE NEXT LEVEL OF PERSONAL PRODUCTIVITY!

We have worked though a formidable list of essentials in the effort to raise personal productivity. Congratulations if you have taken these elements into your consciousness. You will, of course, need months and months of practice before you have them all mastered, but at least you are on your way.

Now there is more to confront. (I never promised anyone that becoming a success in small business management was painless, did I?) I have a second list for you to tackle. These items too are important if you are to put in place a comprehensive system of managing your own and your people's time and energy through each work period.

On my second list are these elements:

- Procrastination
- Interruptions
- Stop/Change/Start
- Meetings
- Delegation

Take a deep breath (or maybe a whole series of deep breaths), and let's go on!

Curing Procrastination

The primary cause of procrastination is fear. When you put off accomplishing a task you have set for yourself (or that circumstances dictate you should do), you are afraid of something happening or not happening. You fear that when you complete the tax forms, you will end up owing the IRS money. You are afraid that the new product you are developing will not bring in its costs once you put it on the market. This might sound a bit silly to some of you, but there is also a fear of success that is fairly common—although, typically, buried deep in the subconscious. What's behind this fear? Perhaps low self-esteem tells you that you are not "worthy" of being successful. Or trepidation about the demands of success—how to handle pressures from family, for instance—makes you avoid success.

Behind procrastination, on some level, is the belief that if you put off deciding or doing, the outcome will be better or the fear will be less or the problem will go away on its own. You are telling yourself a lie. And this lie is usually well concealed, as I discussed in Step 6 (Build Strong Business Habits). The most common lie is that putting off the action won't matter. We tell ourselves, "Oh, there's really no difference in whether I get this done today or tomorrow." But deep down we know it's a lie.

The costs of procrastination can be enormous. This one undermining habit can torpedo all your other efforts to build a successful business. Because of procrastination you may *never* reach many of the goals you have set. And there are other costs. These include things such as depressed self-esteem; lowered confidence; greater stress, including possibly feelings of being overwhelmed by what remains to be done; lack of balance; diminished peace of mind; and loss of productive time.

Take a moment now and write down in the spaces below the costs to you personally and to your business when you procrastinate. Try to be as specific as you can.

Costs of my (our) procrastination:

_____

_____

_____

_____

Procrastination is not just any occasion when you put off making a decision or taking an action. It is important to distinguish between times when you are thoughtfully delaying an action because you believe you need more information or the time is not yet right to act, and times when you are lying to yourself and dragging your feet when you should be moving ahead. Only you can make this distinction. Making this judgment accurately will require keen self-awareness and brutal honesty.

Here are eight steps you can take to overcome either an incident or a pattern of procrastination.

1. You must become more aware of your procrastination: How do you talk to yourself when you are procrastinating? How do you convince yourself that a delay is

justifiable? How do you put things out of sight or out of mind? You must almost say to yourself, literally, "I am procrastinating here. This is not good for business. I have to make a breakthrough and start getting this done."
2. Calculate for yourself the costs of procrastination in each instance.
3. Uncover the lie behind each occasion of procrastination. What have you been telling yourself? "It's not important," "This can wait," "Other things have to take priority."
4. Define the worst-case outcome—that which you fear the most and that which, in all probability, is keeping you from acting. "I'll owe more taxes," "If the product fails, we'll lose our investment."
5. Resolve that you will not let procrastination bog you down.
6. Take some action, even if you have to jump into the middle of something; even if the action may seem to you insignificant, such as putting tax forms up on the edge of your desk, or writing yourself a big reminder of the action to be taken and posting it where you cannot avoid seeing it, etc.
7. Follow up by taking one step after another until the action is completed. Break up the process into a series of small but identifiable steps.
8. Reward yourself when you have completed the process. Treat yourself (and your spouse or a friend) to a movie, a round of golf, a massage, or whatever else you find is a motivating reward.

Handling Interruptions

There you are in your office, intensely focused on an urgent project for a client. Ideas for improving the project are rolling through your mind. Then, BRRRING! It's the phone. Should you answer it? You've been expecting one or two important calls, and you don't want to play phone tag. So . . . you pick up the phone.

On the other end is one of your vendors, asking for clarification on an order. You have to dig through some files and track down the information she has requested. It takes you two or three minutes. You were glad to be able to resolve the vendor's questions, but you find when you turn back to your project that . . . "Where was I? Just what were those refinements I was thinking of?" Your mind is a blank.

What can you do to protect a focused and productive period of the day from being splintered into pieces by a jarring interruption? Let's look at the two basic forms of interruptions: (1) the telephone and (2) the walk-in (employee, client, visitor, supplier, whomever).

The telephone. When you start a work session, decide ahead of time if you can be interrupted. That is to say, before the phone even rings, know whether you are going to take the call. If you have decided that you will take calls, have in mind some quick phrase to invite people to get back to you or a way of promising to return their call if the matter they are calling about can wait. You might also have in mind which kinds of calls you will allow yourself to take (from a client, yes; from a supplier, no, etc.). If you don't have an assistant to screen your calls, Caller ID is a huge help. You might find it one of your wisest phone service investments.

Set the tone of each conversation right away. If the matter can wait, jump right in with "I'm sorry, I'm very tied up just at the moment. Can I get back to you in . . . a half hour, an hour, tomorrow?" Set a definite phone appointment with the person, and schedule it in your agenda or planner, just as you would a face-to-face meeting. (This only works if you've earned people's trust by returning calls when you said you would. Otherwise, not wanting to play telephone tag, they will insist on talking with you while they have you on the phone. Do you see how good habits lead to good results?)

If you need to get some phone calls out of the way to clear the deck for intense creative working time, you might consider sending e-mails or faxes instead of getting on the phone.

The walk-in. Schedule open-door time. During these periods, anyone who wants to see you, employee or visitor, is free to come in. Keep to the schedule if you want people to trust you.

Another good way to defuse staff interruptions is to schedule regular short meeting times where any routine problem or request can be aired. If you do this on a daily basis—and 15 minutes is usually enough with a small working group—you will find you have fewer interruptions during the day.

Some managers leave their office door open just an inch. This communicates to one and all that, yes, you may interrupt me, but it had better be important!

Stop/change/start. When you are interrupted, consciously say to yourself, "Stop!" You do this so that you will not go on thinking about what you were doing when you were interrupted, you will let go of it for the moment.

Then say to yourself, "Change!" This signals to your mind that you are going to be shifting gears.

Finally, tell yourself, "Start!" This is your green light to focus on the matter that is being brought to your attention through the interruption. See if this isn't a major help when you suddenly have to refocus your attention.

MEETINGS

Meetings can be either your most productive time or your biggest time waster. You get to choose which. Fortunately, entrepreneurs spend less time in meetings than their corporate counterparts. Even so, a few tips for meetings are in order.

To make each meeting more productive:

- Have a specific purpose for the meeting.
- Send a written agenda to all participants well ahead of the meeting, so they can prepare comments and questions.
- Have a person in charge (sometimes called a "facilitator").
- Stick to the agenda.
- Put off new topics until a future meeting.
- Communicate and deliberate all information gathered by each participant regarding the issue at hand.
- Respect the ideas and comments of all present.
- Limit discussion to the essentials.
- Work toward a decision (even if the decision is that "we need more information before we decide.").
- Make a commitment to act.

In sum, use the best meeting system I know: state the issue, present relevant information, decide, and act.

Delegation

Delegation is critical to growing a business. First, however, you have to know what cannot be delegated.

As the owner-manager of a business, you should not delegate things such as a final decision on overall goal setting and planning. Don't delegate the responsibility for creating the culture—the climate—in which your business will develop.

Quite rarely you may be able to delegate responsibility for the overall financial management if you are positive that someone you can trust absolutely will do it better than you can do it yourself.

Important matters you can delegate are: daily operations, marketing, sales, customer service, bookkeeping, inventory control, and premises and equipment maintenance. Ask yourself right now: "What do I want to maintain total control of? And what am I willing to delegate?"

Not limiting yourself to just the categories of operations cited above, answer the following questions.

■ ■ ■ ■
I will keep primary responsibility for the following functions:
_____
_____
_____
_____

■ ■ ■ ■
I will delegate the following responsibilities:
_____
_____
_____
_____

The next step is to take the plunge and actually delegate the responsibilities you said you would delegate. Don't waffle on it. Do it! Often this is easier said than done. Most entrepreneurs start as solo operators of their venture and do almost everything from riding herd on the books to sweeping the floor. As you grow, doing it all becomes craziness. Delegation is your path to sanity.

Once you have delegated a responsibility, back off. Resist the temptation (which may, in some cases, be very strong) to micromanage. This does not mean that you should not set goals for those to whom you've delegated a responsibility or that you should have no input into the process. It does mean that you should let the person do his or her job, and do it in a personal fashion.

Stay in touch with team members to whom you've passed a baton, and get regular reports on their activities. Be ready with advice when they seem to be stuck or when they want your attention. They'll appreciate both the assurance that you are there when you need them, and the assurance that, in the normal course of things, you will give them the space they need to make their own decisions.

Does that sound like a workable system?

We'll talk more about systems in the next step, bringing along the skills we've learned up to now.

TEST YOUR INNER GAME EQ: PRODUCTIVITY

Rate yourself from 1 (weak) to 5 (strong) on how much each statement reflects your current state. Go with the first answer that comes to mind as you read each statement. Circle the number that best represents your capacity in each quiz item.

1. I am aware of my personal productivity.   1 2 3 4 5

2. I know productivity comes from managing my actions.   1 2 3 4 5

3. I notice when I am most productive.   1 2 3 4 5

4. I observe what makes me most productive.   1 2 3 4 5

5. I am improving my personal productivity.   1 2 3 4 5

Productivity total _____

Evaluate Your Business Systems

> The art of life lies in constant readjustment to our surroundings
> —Okakura Kakuzo

The first law of ecology, according to Barry Commoner, the well-known environmental scientist, is that "everything is related to everything." Guess what? This is a fundamental reality in business too—though one that escapes many entrepreneurs. How often do we say something like, "A chain is only as strong as its weakest link," or "You touch a drumskin in one spot and it reverberates all over." Yet small business people frequently act as if they don't believe this is true for their venture.

There is no getting away from it, though: Production affects accounting and sales policies. Those matters affect advertising (and vice versa). Your use of all communications media, both internal and external (telephone, fax, memos to staff, bulletin boards, the company newsletter, etc.), impact on such things as efficiency, morale, and productivity.

We're talking here about systems. Systems are at the heart of how you run your business. They are structured ways of approaching problems, coming to decisions, and carrying out policies—whatever you use, in other words, to *get things done.* One way of configuring your systems is to divide them into three groups: technical (equipment), operational (processes), and human (people-to-people relations). These three groups might—imperfectly—be thought of as three meshing gears. If any system is off track, obviously it will wreck the meshing process and throw your whole business askew.

SEE THE BIG PICTURE

Systems thinking views organizations as a whole. No longer do you see each function—production, sales, accounting, etc.—as an independent unit, but rather you view them all as parts of one unified operation. Everywhere you look, you see interrelatedness. And you start to realize that your venture does not exist in isolation from the world outside it, but that it is part of a larger system, a larger "whole" called the marketplace.

Peter Senge, in his path-breaking book *The Fifth Dimension,* suggests that the reason we focus on parts, to the detriment of seeing the whole, is that "from a very early age, we are taught to break problems apart, to fragment the world." The downside to this, according to Senge, is "we can no longer see the consequences of our actions; we lose our intrinsic sense of connection to a larger whole."

When you begin to think in systems, begin to see those gears meshing as your venture develops, you get a clearer sense of the big picture. The challenge is that you will now be aware of how each component within your operation affects, in some way or another, all the other components. This may be somewhat frightening. Nonetheless, it is better that you come to grips with what is an important reality than that through ignoring it you find your business on the verge of collapse.

Unfortunately for them, many small business owners do not think very deeply about what systems they will need to support the growth and goals they set for themselves. Usually, systems are created haphazardly as a need appears, and little thought is given to how one system affects others.

In this step, you will learn to understand, design, and analyze the functions of systems.

WHY ARE SYSTEMS SO IMPORTANT?

As the very machinery that makes your business operate, systems are like the punch press that stamps out the widget. They also are what drive your day-to-day operations.

Most important of all, systems affect behavior. One set of structures—such as policies for employees, a crisp dress code, and cordial customer service demeanors and level of politeness—will encourage one set of behavior. A slacker policy in this area will encourage a completely different—and less desirable—form of behavior. Senge notes: "When put in the same system, people, however different, tend to produce similar results."

Consider this metaphor: If you take healthy fish and put them into a dirty fish tank, they will get sick and quite probably die. The environment in which you place the fish is not conducive to keeping them lively and performing as fish. Putting healthy and potentially productive people in a toxic business environment, such as one where bitter criticism is the order of the day, will not encourage them to perform at their best. In fact, they may limp along in marginal fashion until finally the business itself keels over and dies. You may have had the right people all along, but without the right human resources system, it's all to no avail.

Instead of playing catch-up—reacting to breakdowns in systems—or putting the blame on the people operating the systems, you can learn to generate higher levels of productivity, and keep your error quotient low, by putting in place the right systems in the first place, and keeping them well maintained.

UNDERSTAND DYNAMIC COMPLEXITY IN YOUR SYSTEMS

Whenever you change one part of a system, everything else is affected. What is more, the rate of change often takes on mind-boggling velocity.

Dynamic complexity is different from what most people think of when they consider complexity. The most common variety of complexity is detail complexity. This means simply having a lot of things to manage all at once—staff, products, sales mechanisms, accounting mechanisms, equipment, customer demands. Detail complexity is the basic perspective of accounting: many details represented in tabular fashion on balance sheets or financial projections. Algebra is the math for detail complexity.

Dynamic complexity also involves many items being managed simultaneously, but here each item is *in motion*—in a process of dynamic evolution. Even the rates of change are changing.

Consider the market forces in your industry, be it landscaping, market research, or hosting Web sites. The mix of dynamic complexity includes customers—a large group of people with different tastes, and those tastes are evolving. Then there is the competition—a group of businesses like yours, each trying to perceive and satisfy the tastes and demands of the customers. On another side of the equation are vendors and suppliers who are trying to get or keep your business just as you try to acquire or keep your customers' business. And there you are in the middle, trying to figure out a strategy that will give you an edge.

The math for dynamic complexity is calculus. This is the math of analyzing rates of change and representing those rates as a function. In order to work with calculus you have to have algebra as a base.

A common example of what happens in the whirlwind of dynamic complexity is the developing and launching of a new product. If the product is truly original to you, all sorts of dynamics are set in motion by its launch. Suppliers must be tipped off to provide you with adequate amounts of materials needed for the product's composition. Customers must be attracted to the product and sold on trying it. And, of course, you must brace for competitors jumping into the market and trying to cut down your lead. But you don't even need to have a new product for all these things to happen: a significant upgrade of an existing product, or even a highly innovative way of advertising a product, will generate all the same effects.

Coming up with the "right" answer to a business problem in a context of dynamic complexity is like trying to connect with a fastball rocketing in toward you, the batter, at 90 mph. While this might sound like an overwhelming challenge, there are indeed mind-sets and techniques that can help you sharpen your batting eye. In fact, systems thinking, which developed out of electronic and mechanical engineering, is designed specifically to meet this challenge.

The very first change in viewpoint that systems thinking calls on us to make is to stop tinkering with parts of the system as if they were autonomous or independent. Instead, start seeing and dealing with the whole of your operation, and account for the interrelatedness of all the parts.

What frequently happens when we focus on solving a problem in one part of our operation, without linking that solution to its repercussion on all the other parts, is that we lose sight of the big picture—and end up creating more problems.

Jack is the owner-manager of a three-person graphic arts firm. Jack hasn't given himself a raise for a while and he has noticed that the competition charges more than he does. So he decides to raise his rates. Most of his customers accept the rate change. Suddenly, however, Jack finds that customers who have stayed with him are demanding more service and higher quality. Meanwhile, his two employees, one an accomplished graphic artist and the other a secretary–artist trainee, begin to complain of being overworked and suggest it would be good if he hired someone part-time or else farmed out a portion of the work. What did Jack overlook in raising his rates? He forgot to factor into the rate hike a potential customer demand for a higher grade of work, which would translate into pressure on existing staff and a demand for relief through adding staff or subcontracting.

What Jack may have done as well, without realizing it, is move his graphic operation "up market." He may have abandoned a price niche in the market that his firm had comfortably occupied and put the firm in a different niche; now even the competition is different—and so are customer expectations. The new target market might call for a new marketing plan, including new kinds of advertising.

There's nothing wrong with moving "up market"—so long as you do it consciously. When you make such a move haphazardly, hardly realizing what you are doing to yourself and your staff, you could find yourself in turbulent water swimming for your life.

Adopting a systems thinking approach runs counter to the entrepreneurial notion—which is a myth anyway—that as a business founder and manager, you are running your own independent business over which you have total control. The realistic view is that forces outside your control have plenty of impact on what happens in your venture, and it is best to be fully aware of them and ready to factor them into decisions you make in an effort to stay healthy as a business and grow.

SEE YOUR BUSINESS AS A MOTION PICTURE—NOT A SNAPSHOT

Another important viewpoint to adopt is that of seeing changes as a motion picture rolling by on a screen, rather than as a snapshot frozen in time. In other words, step back and view everything in motion in and around your operation as a dynamic process. This is hardest to do when changes are incremental and slow. Such changes are nonetheless critical to track if you are to adjust your business to keep pace.

Many businesses fail because they let gradual change creep up on them and wipe them out. The owner-managers of these firms focus too intently on the day-to-day minicrises— the new competitor that appears, the employee that suddenly announces he wants to quit, the latest price increase in supplies. Meanwhile, at a much slower pace, important changes may be building in your industry. Missing them, or underrating them, could cost you everything.

The American auto industry provides an example of such myopia. In the early 1960s the Big Three manufacturers dominated the U.S. market. Japanese auto makers had managed only a 4 percent share. When Japan increased its share to 10 percent in 1967, the Big Three took scant notice.

And they did not adjust their models or marketing either when in 1974 the Japanese share had risen to 15 percent. Not until the early 1980s, when the Japanese market share had climbed to a hefty 21 percent, did American automakers react seriously.

Year by year, the changes in the auto industry were not dramatic. Over time, however, they added up to market challenges of the highest importance. This sort of thing can happen in any sector of the economy—including yours.

Small, incremental change that goes unnoticed (or inadequately noticed) by an entrepreneur can be more lethal to the business than the one-time major or dramatic shakeup. When entrepreneurs lose sight of patterns of change in their marketplace, they are losing touch with what is important—and courting disaster.

THE FEEDBACK LOOP IN BUSINESS SYSTEMS

The basic mechanism of any system—business or otherwise—is the feedback loop. The feedback will be there whether we realize it or not, whether we take advantage of it or not. In other words, businesses that end in bankruptcy could have seen "the handwriting on the wall," if they had known where to look or were not indulging in denial of the evidence. Feedback will show us either that what we are doing is taking hold (is working or being accepted, by customers, staff, or whomever) or is provoking resistance. We ignore feedback at our peril.

Informal feedback will come to us even if we do not consciously attempt to build feedback loops into our systems: Employees either will or will not be as productive as you hoped—or as their résumés or skills would have led you to believe. You'll have repeat customers or you won't. Suppliers will offer you larger discounts for your faithfulness in using their services and paying promptly—or they won't.

However, you may indeed want to structure feedback more formally. Typically, you can do this by deciding you want to measure things, such as customer flow, month-by-month revenues, or employee productivity, or else by taking surveys. Some of the best surveys are oral and very low key. For instance, at the end of a meeting with a client a marketing consultant might simply ask, "Rachel, you've been relying on us to help chart your marketing plan for ten months now. How are we doing? What do you think have been the biggest pluses and the biggest minuses of our service? What could we be doing better?" If your rapport with this client has been good, chances are you will get some excellent feedback in response to these questions.

There is merit, too, to more highly structured ways of soliciting feedback, such as having interviewers buttonhole clients on their way out of a business and ask a list of ten specific questions. Or by doing telephone surveys of customers. I happen to like the off-the-cuff direct questioning approach I describe above. You can do something similar with your employees in periodic low-key performance reviews—not the kind you schedule six weeks in advance, but the informal, "Hey, have you got a minute, let's chat," type of interaction. During these little pauses, over coffee or just standing in someone's doorway, you can get a sense of both how the employee is performing (in his or her own estimation) and what the employee may like and dislike about the job, the company facilities, atmosphere, and personal interactions during the workday.

In terms of feedback on your ways of doing business, here's a metaphor that we all can readily appreciate: There you are, already under the shower, and suddenly the water feels too hot! What do you do? You step back and turn the faucet toward "cold." But you go too far. Now the water feels too cold. So you jump back again, and keep adjusting back and forth, until you get the temperature just right for you. Now you can take your shower in blissful comfort. Business is very much the same. We may swing erratically, for example, between doing no advertising at all, and then launching an advertising blitz. When the blitz campaign brings in unsatisfactory results, we shut down our advertising completely—again! All the while, a steadier, more moderately budgeted, advertising campaign may have been what we really needed. To be effective, advertising must be steady, consistent, and long term.

Use Patience in Absorbing Feedback

With our typical American propensity for the quick fix, we hanker for feedback to hit us in the face and then propel us in the direction of making the needed adjustments right away. Some feedback loops, however, require that we be patient.

The most obvious example of this is customer service. The way you treat your customers will always come back to affect your business. But the effects do not usually come back immediately. Sometimes it takes months, even years, for the effects of your customer service policies to loop back either to help you or to haunt you.

Thus, an important element in any feedback loop is the waiting period, or delay. Not understanding the delay time makes it quite hard to determine how to properly adjust a customer service tactic (such as telling clothing-store clerks to smile at browsing customers first, then speak to them a minute or two later).

Let's return for a moment to the shower example. The reason many people fail to adjust the shower water temperature to their liking on the first try is that they have a poor understanding of the delay in the feedback loop of the shower mechanism. Some showers take about ten seconds to produce a steady stream of water at a given temperature after a user adjustment. If you wait only three or four seconds before you readjust the temperature, you are adjusting before the temperature change is complete.

The same impatience shows up in business. Without taking the time and trouble to understand what the proper delay is in a loop, owner-managers may make changes almost continuously (in customer service or in another system), trying to "get it right." They are most unlikely to learn from their mistakes if they do not have the patience to wait to see the true effects of whatever change they install.

Hiring an employee and putting that employee in your production systems, using a new business strategy, or launching a marketing campaign, all come packaged with built-in feedback loops. It may take months, or in some cases even years, for you to know whether these decisions were effective or not. And yes, it is difficult to gauge the right time frame for being sure you have enough feedback to evaluate your decision. At the very least, however, whenever you are on the verge of making a change in your systems, you need to consider how long you should reasonably expect to wait to amass enough feedback to appraise the results. This could range from a portion of a day to weeks or months.

Small businesses have an advantage here: their businesses, and therefore their systems, are smaller and less complex than the systems of giant corporations. Usually this will mean that the effects of your feedback loops will be felt sooner.

Reinforcing Feedback

The generator of growth in business is a phenomenon we call "the reinforcing feedback process." In any situation where you are experiencing growth in your venture, you may be 100 percent sure that—whether you consciously realize it or not—the reinforcing feedback process is at work.

Here's how it works: Small changes are fed into a system, working out well, thus confirming that introducing them was a good idea, and then these same changes get reinforced and relaunched into the system. Every time you reintroduce a successful item back into the system, its positive effect on your business is amplified.

A simple example would be a vending display. Beth and Adam run a bookstore and have just ordered a calendar they think is especially engaging. They bought a large quantity because they believe in the item. However, it is not moving from the shelves, so Beth constructs a point of purchase display and sets it up right inside the front door. Suddenly the calendars begin to fly off the rack. Adam is then able to reorder calendars and keep them on display up front, and the store's sales continue to go well.

There are other names for this phenomenon—the snowball effect, the bandwagon effect, or where people skills are concerned the Pygmalion effect. (The Pygmalion effect is aptly portrayed in the musical comedy *My Fair Lady*. Eliza Doolittle begins to speak correct London English because of the expectation and coaching of Professor Higgins. This is a syndrome in which people get what they expect to get and is also known as the "self-fulfilling prophecy.")

You may hire a person as a management trainee because you believe she is really sharp. You therefore devote a lot of time and energy to training her. Your new hire responds enthusiastically to the training and begins to demonstrate high-quality management skills. You yourself then feel validated in your choice of this woman's great potential for managing staff, and so you shower even more attention upon her, as well as rewards for progress achieved. She responds to this with even greater energy and attention to her work. And on and on it can go.

The reinforcing process can work either upward or downward. A downward cycle occurs when you go into something expressing lots of doubts, or holding back some of your energy because you are not confident of success. Because Denise is not sure a new investing package will be attractive to the clientele of her financial planning agency, she does not develop it as thoughtfully as she might otherwise have done. Indeed, the program shows only meager results. So Denise refrains from fine-tuning it. Results begin to drop even more, and she puts less and less energy into working the program. Finally, the project fails. "I knew it!" she tells herself (and maybe others). "I doubted this would ever work and I was right."

I don't mean to claim that all the results produced in your business result directly from whether your expectations were positive or negative. Nonetheless, your expectations do have great impact on how each tactic or campaign unfolds.

One downside to the reinforcing feedback process is that it can encourage runaway growth. And out-of-control growth can kill a business faster than zero growth. So, while a reinforcing system is highly useful, it must be controlled. Fortunately, another system exists that can accomplish just that.

Balancing Feedback

For better or for worse, balancing feedback stabilizes growth around some ideal point for the system. This system is in play on occasions when you may be trying to "rev up" your business, trying all sorts of innovations, and nothing seems to make any difference. Your business volume stays at the same level. What's going on? The answer is that the system has its own agenda.

Whenever you perceive balancing feedback at work, you can be assured that there is a goal driving it. This may not be a goal you consciously chose. "What!?!" some of you may be thinking. "How can a system be organized around a goal that I did not consciously choose?" The key word here is "consciously." If you, in your subconscious, are fearful of being "too successful," or of having to manage a large group of people, or of being responsible for the financial well-being of numerous employees, or of having your business steal you away from your family life, you will feed into the system stop-and-go mechanisms. These mechanisms will, in effect, adjust the system to achieve the balance—something I also term "an implicit goal"—that you subconsciously seek.

This balancing process is at work in your heating and air-conditioning system. That system automatically seeks a comfort zone. The system activates mechanisms to bring the heat up or turn on the air-conditioning in reaction to cold or heat bearing down on your house from the outside. The balancing system in your business operates in much the same way. You can see how the reinforcing and balancing systems have been operating in your business to bring you to the level of success you have achieved thus far. And I trust that these insights will help you more consciously, and realistically, plan for future growth.

USE SYSTEMS THINKING IN YOUR BUSINESS

To install systems thinking in your business planning, you first must recognize how you got the patterns now in place. Because writing things down is so much more powerful than just thinking about them, use the lines below to answer.

> "In what ways have I organized my business to result in the behavior patterns that I can now observe?"
>
> _____
> _____
> _____
> _____
> _____
> _____

Now identify the feedback loops operating in your business. An example would be: "We hold a focus group of customers selected at random every two months and provide them with gift certificates to use in our store in exchange for their candid comments on our customer service, display, variety of merchandise, pricing, and other factors."

These answers should give you much to ponder. By carefully considering how things are going now, and determining what additional or nuanced modes of operations you need in order to achieve better results, you will find yourself pointed in the best direction to upgrade your present systems.

> Using the lines below, identify "What feedback loops can I pinpoint as operating in my business?"
>
> _____
> _____
> _____
> _____
> _____
> _____
> _____
> _____
> _____
> _____

Next you need to identify those goals or agendas whose source very likely lies deep within your own psyche—the way you think and feel, the way your mental models are set and operate. A few examples are fear of success, unwillingness to take responsibility for more employees, and fear of getting into financial considerations that are too complicated or challenging.

Now you have (1) identified the systems currently at work in your business, and (2) the feedback loops attached to each system (whether or not you attached them consciously). The next step is to identify the implicit goals operating in your systems. Then you will be ready to create adjustments.

"What implicit goals—or hidden agendas—might be at work in my (our) business?" Answer using the lines below:

_____
_____
_____
_____
_____
_____
_____
_____

ACHIEVING LEVERAGE IN YOUR BUSINESS SYSTEMS

The way you make progress is through incremental (often quite small) adjustments in your systems. I call these adjustments "strategic actions."

Everything you have read thus far in this step (and, indeed, in the entire book) has been a foundation for building your business through achieving leverage. Peter Senge puts it cogently when he writes: "The bottom line of systems thinking is leverage—seeing where actions and changes in structure can lead to *significant, enduring improvements.*"

Aiming for giant strides, to my way of thinking, is not the best way to grow your business. You can take giant strides later—after you've had some practice spelling out some small steps for yourself and your people, and then actually achieving them. Employing the processes described here, these three businesses used small steps to build:

1. *A small restaurant.* Analysis shows that the premises are being inadequately utilized for the market demand that is present. Solution: Add breakfast and create a buffet line for dinner (while keeping menu items available in limited quantities). Price the breakfast and dinner buffet attractively to increase customer flow.
2. *A small accounting service.* Analysis shows that customers would like more than strict accounting. They need counseling toward the securing of SBA and other loan packages, and introductions to bank officers with whom they might work. Solution: Have one accountant study SBA loan packaging. Have another make the rounds of all the town's leading banks and promote in-depth, personal relationships with loan officers. Using these strengths, develop a brochure to present these services to the firm's clientele.
3. *A market research firm.* Analysis shows that there has been high turnover among staff sent out to conduct interviews. These positions have been a fill-in for many job seekers, and consequently those doing interviews are not engaging enough passersby or attentive enough to ensure that quality research results. Solution: Motivate interviewers through higher salary and bonus, and also cross-train them in office tasks, such as survey analysis and report writing for clients, to make them feel more professional and "part of the team."

Frequently, steps even smaller than those above may be in order. Staff in an office operation might be willing to start at 8 AM instead of 8:30 AM, for instance, if they could then choose the option of:

- Longer breaks
- Extended lunch hour
- Going home early

This slight change—which would have no effect on the office's operations—could result in a significantly greater sense of freedom for staff and appreciation of management.

> Your final assignment in this chapter is to use the lines below to *hypothesize two or three changes that you might consider in your current operations.*
>
> _____
> _____
> _____
> _____
> _____
> _____

With heightened knowledge of business systems, you are now ready to *energize* your work environment.

TEST YOUR INNER GAME EQ: SYSTEMS

■ ■ ■ ■ ■

Rate yourself from 1 (weak) to 5 (strong) on how much each statement reflects your current state. Go with the first answer that comes to mind as you read each statement. Circle the number that best represents your capacity in each quiz item.

1. I am aware of my business
   systems—or lack of them.   1 2 3 4 5

2. I understand the components
   of systems.   1 2 3 4 5

3. I notice the functioning of my
   business systems.   1 2 3 4 5

4. I see how my systems contribute
   to my business.   1 2 3 4 5

5. I am working to improve my
   business systems.   1 2 3 4 5

■ ■ ■ ■ ■

Systems total _____

Energize Your Work Environment

> We shape our buildings, and then our
> buildings shape us.
> —Winston Churchill

You enter a department store and look around. Lighting, wall tones, counter displays, and polished natural wood floors blend to create a mood—a mood that you find agreeable. You like what you see and what you feel. The way the management has chosen to light and decorate the store translates into your feeling glad you are there, and also feeling better about yourself. It isn't always something you can immediately put your finger on, but how many times haven't you found yourself saying, "I like the feel of this place."

Other businesses have had the opposite effect, haven't they? Perhaps the walls had that washed-out, please-paint-me-soon look; or the lighting was either too bright or too weak. Or maybe the displays were unimaginative or even cluttered. "Let me out of here, quick," you said to yourself.

If lighting, decor, and other design elements can have such an impact on you as a visitor or customer, imagine the effect those same elements have on people who must report to work in those environments five days a week. In brief, the environment in which you work is extremely important to the morale and productivity of both you as owner-manager and to your coworkers.

What does it feel like to be in your work environment? Look around you. Notice your current work atmosphere: the lighting you have (natural and otherwise); the colors and styles of painted, papered, or paneled walls; the look and functionality of furniture and equipment; and so forth.

Take in the ensemble, and then focus on your feelings. What sort of feelings does the overall effect trigger in you? Write those feelings below.

> My work atmosphere generates feelings of:
> _____
> _____
> _____
> _____

You may have to focus extra hard to coax out your true feelings. That is because you have been spending your work days in your current environment—perhaps for years—and really seeing what is around you may take some effort.

MEASURE YOUR ENERGY LEVELS

Positive atmospheres tend to energize people. Washed-out or dull atmospheres tend to drag people down.

One way to judge an atmosphere, therefore, is by noticing whether you feel energized or drained while you are in it. Natural sunlight (such as we can enjoy during a walk in the park), soothing colors, cleanliness, and tasteful wall decorations all help to energize us. Ceilings, walls, and floors that are peeling or splotchy, poor light, and an unkempt appearance will cloud our mood. And we will actually feel less like getting any work done.

On a scale of 1 to 5, what energy level would you say that your current work atmosphere promotes?

1   2   3   4   5

If you gave your workplace a score of three or less, what could you change to improve the atmosphere and thus increase the energy levels of yourself and your people?

> Write your changes below:
> _____
> _____
> _____
> _____
> _____

MAKE YOUR WORKPLACE WARM AND FRIENDLY

All the best organizational tools, beautiful colors and textures for walls, window dressings, and floors, cannot make a workplace sparkle if the psychological mood is dour. Fears, jealousies, petty rivalries—which may include snubbing or put-down behaviors—and other "political" elements will color your place stormcloud gray.

You as owner-manager are responsible for establishing the right working mood for everybody who works for you or with you, and for your clients or customers too. In many cases the hard-driving, bottom-line mentality of entrepreneurs who are pushing themselves and their people for fast growth spawns brusqueness or other forms of insensitivity to people issues.

Watch yourself carefully—and listen to the feedback you will inevitably receive from those with whom you work on a regular basis. Some of this feedback may be indirect—such as people demonstrating a reluctance to bring up sticky problems for fear your temper may boil over or you may chastise them for not finding a solution themselves.

Another common problem is that while you yourself may be treating people courteously and fairly, somewhere in the ranks two or more employees are sniping at each other or talking behind each other's backs. Whenever someone who works for you is being trashed by a coworker, there is a disruption of the ideal atmosphere for putting out your product or serving your customers.

Who's responsible for detecting such debilitating rivalries and re-creating the atmosphere so that harmony is restored? You are. In certain cases, especially in larger operations and where there is a budget to support the process, calling in a consultant who is an expert in conflict resolution may be your best bet.

A tactic that will go far in generating happy vibes in your workplace is to "catch people in the act of doing something right," as Ken Blanchard and Spencer Johnson suggest in *The One Minute Manager.*

When you as the owner-manager start recognizing people positively, others will catch on and imitate the tactic. Praise as a management tool, in other words, is contagious.

Acknowledgment works best when you do it just to brighten someone's day and give praise where praise is due. Don't be calculating about praising, figuring on a certain increase in production because you're using the technique. Good things will happen on their own. You don't have to quantify everything.

YOUR WORKPLACE IS ATTRACTIVE, BUT IS IT ORDERLY?

Spanking new desks and up-to-date equipment may help you and your people feel better about getting your work done, but what if all you do is cover every surface with disheveled heaps of paper and sheer junk?

An office or work site where things are kept in disarray will drain the energy right out of you. Instead of being able to lay your hands on a file in five seconds, you may spend five minutes. And five minutes more for the next file you need. It all adds up.

Those of you inclined to be pack rats, beware! If you can hardly get the car into your garage at home, or your attic is creaking under the weight of countless crates and boxes, you may be doing something similar at work.

Plug in your awareness. Look around you and see what you have created. Count the costs. And determine how you can alter your mind-sets toward more efficient storing and sorting of essentials. The junk? Get rid of it.

One caveat: Some people actually thrive on a chaotic atmosphere. A squeaky clean environment, full of neatnik commandments about "keeping everything in order," will drive this breed crazy. If you are truly one of that small number who do better managing your work by fishing things out of stacks on the floor, make a conscious decision to stay with what has worked best for you up to now and make sure your mess doesn't interfere with others' work and work spaces.

WHAT IS THE PURPOSE OF YOUR WORKPLACE?

List all the activities performed at your workplace to help you create a more ideal—and functional—environment. Some of the activities on your list might be: administration, product development, production, marketing, sales, customer service, market research, partnering, networking, community service (outreach), etc. Now . . . how many of these do you perform in your workplace? How many take place elsewhere, such as "on the road," or at clients' offices or work sites? For example, if you have no walk-in traffic, it really doesn't matter whether you locate in a building with an elevator, an elegant lobby, or convenient parking (unless those accoutrements are important to you and your employees).

Write below activities performed in your workplace:

This is an excellent subject for a meeting of you and your people. If you work alone, but have others come to your office for project development or other work, ask a number of your clients to join you in brainstorming to create the ideal atmosphere for you and them. Remember the architectural principle, "form follows function." In other words, for each activity you put on the list there will be elements to install or upgrade that will result in an optimum functional atmosphere for that purpose. Brainstorm it—then do it. This is an exercise you will not regret!

QUALITY IN YOUR WORK ENVIRONMENT

A friend of mine once worked briefly as an on-the-street reporter for a metropolitan television station. At the beginning of his stint at the station he asked a veteran cameraman, "What kind of clothes should I buy to look right on camera?" The cameraman advised, "Don't bother buying expensive clothes. You can buy clothes that are a bargain if you want to—just so they look good." In other words, TV viewers would not be able to see the fine stitching and the designer labels, only the overall "look."

The same is true of office furniture. You don't have to splurge on furnishing your office. Just take the time to find things that are functional and "look good."

Nonetheless, if you happen to be dealing with a clientele that knows and appreciates high-quality furniture—and knows it when they see it (a law office or an advertising agency might be examples)—it may be wise to pay more or shop better.

Measure your purchases against these four checklist items:

1. Match furnishings with the values and goals of your business.

2. Match furnishings with standards in your industry.
3. Match furnishings with your target customers' expectations.
4. Match furnishings with your budget.

This is not a one-size-fits-all matter. Your furnishings should be distinctively *you* and still make a positive impression on clients or customers. If necessary, enlist the services of a professional decorator. Don't expect to just pass on the responsibility. He or she will interview you at length as to your personal tastes and the statement you wish to make with your office's "look." Using a professional should help meet your needs, on budget, and leave your time free to run your business.

ARRANGE YOUR FURNITURE

Too often furniture is placed in a room without adequate attention to effect, functionality, or traffic flow. Here too, a decorator can help.

Whether you arrange the furniture yourself or use a decorator, you might want to consider Feng Shui, the 3,000-year-old Chinese art of decorating. Feng means wind and Shui means water. Feng Shui creates an order of furnishings in a room to promote the highest levels of energy flow. The energy that Feng Shui attempts to channel is called "Chi" in Chinese. Chi is like the famed "force" in Star Wars.

In the Feng Shui system, clutter is seen as stopping the flow of energy. Therefore this system mandates that you remove as much clutter as possible from your environment. Countertops should be kept free of piles of papers and other materials. Only what you are using at the moment should be on your desk.

What is more, furnishings should be placed in a room starting clockwise at the door in such a way as to represent eight "directions" in your life. These eight are:

1. Career
2. Knowledge
3. Family or health
4. Money
5. Fame or reputation
6. Marriage
7. Children
8. Friends

If your office or main work room is square and the door is at the bottom wall toward the left, the best placement of the desk is on the right wall facing the bottom wall where the door is. Other good locations for the desk are on the left wall facing the door, in the center facing the door, and near the right wall facing the door with the chair back to the right wall.

"Knowledge" could well be where you locate your office library. "Marriage" is where you should hang pictures of your spouse (if you are married) or your special "other." "Friends" is where you might arrange a seating area to talk with clients, especially if, in your value system, you like to count your clients as friends.

Should you be interested in exploring the full range of the Feng Shui approach to decorating, you may want to consult a designer experienced in this style.

Plainly, not everyone will be attracted to Feng Shui—or want to invest the personal and emotional energy into developing a work space according to ancient Chinese principles. So, while Feng Shui has much to recommend it, there are other ways to organize a room.

THE PSYCHOLOGY OF COLORS

Different types of businesses call for different moods, and color creates mood.

Red is fiery and conveys the image of roaring energy. An active and busy color, red is best used in places where you want to encourage action or movement. Some fast-food restaurants have chosen to use red as a principal or accent color. They want you in and out; the message is, "This is a place to eat and then get on with your day; if you want to relax, go somewhere else."

Yellow also packs plenty of energy. Most people relate yellow to the sun: hot and full of power. Put yellow where you want activity, but not to stir up as much activity as red will do.

Calm and clear, blue is a soothing color. Blues encourage relaxation and rest—like a calm sea. Blue works best in places where you want customers or clients to feel they can relax, places such as a health professional's waiting room or a seafood restaurant.

Green is the color most of us identify with nature—with grass, bushes, and trees. Green provides an image of healing and growth, especially growth that is easy and gentle.

Ceilings normally should be white (essential to the efficiency of indirect lighting systems). Sheer white for walls, however, is likely to reduce, rather than increase, workplace productivity—it will be too glaring and distracting. It's better to choose pale shades of other colors, and use beige instead of white, to achieve a pleasant tone conducive to getting work done efficiently.

Not only should we think carefully about the hues we will employ to decorate our work space, but also about the intensity of those same colors. Bright shades, and shades that glitter or shimmer, are high energy and high impact. Not very relaxing. Muted shades and pastels—those in earth tones most of all—are better for creating a low-key environment.

Researchers have identified cultural influences in the way colors are perceived. The fashion industry is always trying to guess what colors will be popular 18 months in the future, the time it takes to develop new fashions and bring them to market. Individuals, too, will have different reactions to various colors, based on their own life experiences and the colors they learned to like as children.

Nonetheless, in general terms it works well to use cool colors such as green or blue where conditions may expose employees to relatively high temperatures. Conversely, warm tones such as cream, ivory, or beige help soften a high-ceilinged or chilly space. They also will compensate for a lack of natural light.

THE EFFECTS OF LIGHTING

The most important overall finding I have seen in research on lighting is that light affects people's health and emotional well being. With good physical health and upbeat mental and emotional health comes better productivity.

John Ott, whose book *Health and Light* sold three million copies, is a staunch proponent of natural or full-spectrum lighting.

Until about five generations ago, we depended on natural light. Then Thomas Edison developed the incandescent lamp.

The incandescent lamp does not produce full-spectrum light like the sun. It has a strong yellow tint and very little of the lower—or blue—end of the spectrum. It also has virtually no ultraviolet light and produces its maximum energy in infrared wavelengths invisible to the human eye.

Fluorescent lighting occupies the other end of the spectrum. It consists mostly of blue light. It is extremely common in industry and offices because it is more efficient than incandescent and not so prone to radiate heat as incandescent bulbs. Fluorescent light is, however, notably harsh on the eyes and is far from ideal for reading.

Ott remarks in his book: "Research has now demonstrated that the full spectrum of daylight is important to stimulate man's endocrine system properly." Side effects of eyestrain and other abnormalities are possible for people who spend a large portion of their day under artificial light.

John Ott has his own type of full-spectrum bulbs called Ott-lite; they come with shields that limit emissions of radiation. I use them myself at home, and I highly recommend them to my clients, readers, and friends.

AVOID "SICK BUILDINGS"

Making buildings airtight to conserve energy has often resulted in harmful side effects to the building's occupants. Noxious chemicals in paints, varnishes, and carpet fibers are sealed into your working atmosphere—never to be mitigated by the airing out of rooms that open windows provide.

Both paints and carpets usually have a plastic or an oil base. Most carpeting in fact is made with formaldehyde, the stuff you may have used in high-school biology class to keep dissected frogs from rotting. It is not good for you if you breathe it into your body.

Older buildings frequently still have asbestos under the floorboards, a dangerous carcinogen. New buildings can have plenty of problems, too. One survey estimates that 30 percent of all new or renovated buildings have toxic substance emissions.

In addition to the substances found in the walls and floors of office buildings, plants, and other workplaces, there can be additional toxic influences stemming from cleaning products, including air fresheners, disinfectants, and rug shampoos; from artificial lighting; and even from such standard equipment as computers, copiers, and particleboard furniture and space dividers.

Obviously, second-hand smoke will affect everyone in the vicinity. For this reason, it's a good idea to make your workplace smoke-free, but also provide congenial areas for smokers to gather during their breaks (smokers will thank you for this!).

Your best bet for maximum productivity is a healthy environment. That means a building as free as possible from harmful chemicals, with windows that open and natural lighting. Check the ventilation system—a good one can work wonders for filtering out noxious vapors and particles.

PLANTS ADD LIFE

Living plants bring nature right indoors. Not only are their appearance and freshness pleasant, but they also make oxygen. Plants are truly a recharging and a revitalizing influence.

If indeed you do have to make do—at least for awhile—working in a "sick" building, plants can be a help. A NASA study found that having one live plant for every 100 square feet of building space provides the ideal amount of oxygen for a healthy environment. By this yardstick, a 3,000-square-foot shop ideally should have 30 plants. And a 6,000-square-foot office should have 60 plants. This is a manageable and affordable number for the tremendous benefit of the good quality of air that plants help generate.

Plants do require attention. However, there are services that rent or sell you the plants and come back regularly to keep them looking great.

Test Your Inner Game EQ: Environment

Rate yourself from 1 (weak) to 5 (strong) on how much each statement reflects your current state. Go with the first answer that comes to mind as you read each statement. Circle the number that best represents your capacity in each quiz item.

1. I am aware of my business environment.   1 2 3 4 5

2. I understand what makes a supportive environment.   1 2 3 4 5

3. I see how my environment can help my business.   1 2 3 4 5

4. I notice when my environment is supportive.   1 2 3 4 5

5. I am making my environment more effective.   1 2 3 4 5

Environment total _____

Achieve Productive Synergy in Your Business

> Think of yourself as on the threshold of unparalleled success. A whole clear, glorious life lies before you.
> —Andrew Carnegie

Earlier in this book I suggested that meeting a business problem with precisely the right answer was akin to a baseball batter connecting with a 90 mph fastball and driving it for a hit. The reason the batter is able to swing the bat and meet the ball as it rockets in toward the plate has to do with *synergy*. His eyes transmit the timing and speed of the ball to the brain, which coordinates an incredible variety of bone and muscle movements in harmony so the batter can hit the ball. Without just the right synergy, the batter would not even be able to swing the bat, much less connect with the little white projectile.

So what exactly is synergy? It is a combination of actions or effects that leads to a total effect that is more than the sum of the parts. Beyond this, the product of synergy often is something that could not have been achieved any other way except for a combination of coordinated efforts or skills. In short, synergy is extremely important to your business.

Years ago Adam Smith, author of the classic *The Wealth of Nations,* gave us one of our better descriptions of synergy in the economic process. He took the simple example of a single woolen coat worn by a day laborer and described it as "the product of the joint labor of a great multitude of work[ers]." Among these he named shepherds, sorters of wool, dyers, spinners, weavers, sewers, transporters, merchants, and others. Without the collaboration of thousands of hands, he said, even those who wore inexpensive garments could not be clothed.

Smith also provided a textbook depiction of synergy when he gave the world his famous pin-factory example. At this factory—which he had personally observed—ten workers were able to manufacture about 48,000 pins per day. They did this by performing a variety of tasks, but in close coordination, one with another. Smith estimated that if any one of the ten had tried to perform all the tasks alone, it was doubtful that this individual, working all day, would have been able to produce more than a single pin. What made the bountiful production of pins possible was a precisely synchronized process where every worker did something specific very well—and did it over and over again throughout the day.

All around us, every day, we can observe instances of synergy: in the flow of traffic through a metropolitan area's expressways and streets, in the gathering and disseminating of world news, and in the bio-diversity evident even in a small patch of parkland where many species of insects and other life forms meet and interact (including providing food for one another).

You already are enjoying the effects of synergy in your business—or else you wouldn't have been able to stay in business at all! What you very probably have not been doing, however, is observing or understanding that synergy. Nor in all likelihood have you been doing anything to fine-tune the synergy and thereby increase your productivity—and your chances for enduring success.

The concept of synergy has roots in medieval theology and in the evolution of the sciences of physiology, biology, and metallurgy. Theologically it dealt with the interactions between Divine will and individual human will. In physiology and medicine, it encapsulated the cooperation of a multitude of human organs in running the body. And in metallurgy it explained the process of many agents working together to achieve the metamorphosis necessary for the production of iron.

Sayings such as "success builds on success" or "the rich keep getting richer" describe the phenomenon of synergy. This is a process that all of us have experienced working in our lives; few of us, however, have given it the label "synergy" or taken the time or trouble to understand the synergistic process in any depth. Now is your chance.

SYNERGY PRODUCES EXPONENTIAL RESULTS

Tracing how synergy produces exponential change, instead of simple linear change, we can learn how to harness similar actions. *Linear change* is like addition of numbers (3+3=6 or 6+3=9). Linear change increases by regular increments. An example would be a person running a cash register for a store. After each week of training and practice, the person would get better, faster, and more accurate (less likely to make an error), until he or she plateaued at some optimum state for operating the cash register.

Exponential change is quite different. It is more like multiplication (3×3=9 or 3×3×3=27). A synergistic approach to initiating a new employee would probably involve cross-training for a variety of tasks. Instead of simply training the person to run the cash register, perhaps you would also train the new employee to serve as host or hostess, do simple bookkeeping, and be able to substitute for other employees in case of absences. Here you have not addition but multiplication of the positive effects the new employee can have on the business' success. If, at the same time, you cross-train all other staff to learn each other's jobs, you multiply still more the positive impact on your business operations.

Exponential growth may start at a small rate (3×3 = only 3 more than 3+3), but the sums keep increasing. The difference between linear and exponential change also may be thought of as the difference between a constant speed (say 30 mph) and acceleration, when you may reach 15 mph after the first second of depressing your car's gas pedal, 30 mph after the third second, and 60 mph after the sixth second.

Astute franchising represents synergistic, or exponential, growth. Kentucky Fried Chicken, at one point, was simply Col. Sanders' Fried Chicken restaurant in Shelbyville, Kentucky (near Louisville). That is, until some businesspeople expert in developing franchises came by, tasted the colonel's cooking, and got him to sign on to a program of expansion that became an American business classic.

APPLY INNER GAME TECHNIQUES TO YOUR BUSINESS—SYNERGISTICALLY!

Applied to the book that you hold in your hands, synergy would come from not just the application of one or two techniques in isolation, but from the simultaneous application—and blending!—of a number of techniques.

Suppose you are researching and writing a business plan. A linear approach might have you wrestling with it yourself, perhaps using one of the popular workbooks or software programs for hammering out a plan. You might be filling in the blanks and not delving deeply into your mind and your emotions, nor reaching out to others for help. Plugging in awareness and attention (laser focusing), however, might surface some of your underlying fears about trusting yourself and an anonymous piece of software. This might lead you to a *mind-set* squirreled away in your inner self that said, "No matter how well I do this plan, the bank is going to reject it." That mind-set has to be faced. Dialogue with a spouse, friends, and a business adviser such as an accountant would be helpful in uncovering the lie behind that mind-set ("I'm never going to be good enough to really succeed in business") and also give you needed support.

Getting in touch with the original desire that motivated you to start a business would give you an additional resource for doing battle with the lie and changing your mind-set. So armed, you are ready to change to a more productive mind-set, one that says something like, "I'm climbing a steep learning curve toward achieving success in my venture; I've already come a good ways, and with a little help from my friends, I can go all the way." This is a synergistic approach to fulfilling your business plan.

Getting feedback on what you have drafted from a variety of counselors (spouse, friends, accountant, lawyer, fellow businesspeople) and blending into your plan the best advice of each will continue to improve your document through synergy. In the end you will have a business plan that has been improved exponentially and is several times more likely to gain approval and lead to success than the plan you might have done by yourself.

Your solo plan might indeed have been rejected by the banker—thus reinforcing your limiting mind-set. Your synergistic plan will either be accepted or will lend itself to relatively simple retailoring for a second try, reinforcing your *new* mind-set—that of making real progress in mastering the learning curve you have set out to conquer.

DISCOVER THE SYNERGY OF LEARNING CURVES

Studying, digesting, and putting into practice the techniques detailed in this book puts you on a learning curve. It's like learning to scale the face of a rocky cliff. At first, it's scary. Then it's discouraging when you come to rough spots and find you need to return to base and start over rather than go forward. Here is where patience and persistence come in. With good coaching and with determination on your part to "never give up," you will gradually master the techniques to scale the wall that leads to the business success you seek.

Remember: All your efforts constitute progress, even if all you learned was what not to do. More likely you discovered inner strengths and outer skills.

Consider the stone cutter who has to hammer a chisel into a stone 100 times before the stone breaks. The first 99 blows leave little physical evidence that the stone is about to split. Then, on the hundredth strike, the stone breaks. Clearly, though, the hundredth strike did not split the stone all by itself. Though no fissure was apparent, something was indeed happening inside the stone with each of the preceding 99 hits. They all were necessary in order for the stone finally to split.

BE AWARE OF SYNERGY

Your business is already the product of synergy. And now that you have become—I hope—considerably more aware of what synergy is and how it operates, focus your attention on evidence of synergy in your business.

Make a list below of processes in which you and your associates are engaged that involve synergy:

_____
_____
_____
_____
_____

Reflect for a moment on the items you have just written down. What have they to do with:

- Your mind-sets? _____
_____

- Your feelings? _____
_____

- Your desires? _____
_____

- Your habits? _____
_____

- Your goals? _____
_____

Has the synergy in these operations been up until now beyond your conscious awareness?

> ▰▰▰▰▰
> Describe how becoming keenly aware of synergy, and focusing your attention on it, could act as a catalyst for improving your business.
> _____
> _____
> _____
> _____
> _____

On another plane, see if you can identify any inconsistency between your original dream, your current goals for your company, and the mind-sets, feelings, and habits on which you are now operating. (For example, perhaps your goal is to become a $2 million company within the next three years, but an examination of your feelings—especially anxieties and fears—about achieving that goal and the habits you currently exhibit—especially those you consider counterproductive—may reveal an important conflict.)

How would using a synergistic combination of the techniques in this book help you to break through to a mode of thinking or operating that would resolve the inconsistency or conflict you may have identified? In other words, what techniques would serve you best, in what order, and in what combination? The techniques you should reflect on here include *awareness* and *attention*, and the ways you consciously

> Clearly write out any inconsistency or conflict that you discover between your dream and your reality:
>
> _____
> _____
> _____
> _____
> _____

own and manage your *mind-sets, feelings, desires, habits* (including *"personal productivity"* or *"time management"*), *systems,* and your *environment.*

> Write your answer below:
>
> _____
> _____
> _____
> _____
> _____
> _____
> _____

DESCRIBE YOUR MIND-SET ABOUT SYNERGY

Some of you may have had trouble with the exercise above; others might have found it comforting—or even exhilarating. Whichever is the case for you, I invite you to focus your awareness on your own mental models or mind-sets. Identify your beliefs about the value of synergy:

- ❏ I am not clear about what it is and how it operates in my business.
- ❏ I get the concept, but it feels scary to apply it.
- ❏ It feels like a real struggle to deliberately apply synergistic thinking to my business—it seems like an awful lot of work.
- ❏ Yes, I understand what you're saying and I'm excited about applying synergistic thinking.

Whichever box(es) you checked (or whatever you wrote after "other"), please take a moment now and expand on your mental model about synergy. Below, define it and comment on how you feel about the model and what you would like to do to change it:

_____
_____
_____
_____
_____

❏ For some time, I have been thinking along the lines you describe and what you say in the book has been very reinforcing to me.

❏ Other _____.

RUNNING YOUR BUSINESS IS A PATH TO SELF-DISCOVERY

How much have you learned about yourself since you began your venture? How have your struggles with starting and developing a competitive business revealed the strengths and weaknesses of your personal makeup (personality, character, intelligence, imagination, values, etc.)?

Whatever state your business is currently in, it is always a reflection of your own self. In fact I would contend that the process of developing and managing a business is one of the greatest paths to self-awareness that our society makes available to us.

What have you learned about yourself through your experiences in business?

Write what you have learned below:
_____
_____
_____
_____

Given the self-knowledge that you have achieved by being in business, and conscious of areas where you are weak, what particular lessons of *The Inner Game of Entrepreneuring* apply most directly to you and to your efforts to achieve your goals for yourself, your family, your employees, and your customers or clients?

▪ ▪ ▪ ▪
List the lessons that most apply to you:
_____
_____
_____
_____
_____
_____

EXPERIENCE PRODUCTIVE CHANGE

Well, here we are, almost at the end of our journey together. Some of you may be saying at this point: I don't know how much I've managed to accomplish. I'm not sure that anything has changed about the way I operate myself or my business. Ah, but remember the stonecutter! You have been making strikes at a piece of granite, and inside the stone, though nothing may yet be evident, molecules are in motion, a process of change has been initiated. Trust me: Anyone who has read this far has been hammering away at the stone. Keep it up! You are working toward a breakthrough—or perhaps any number of breakthroughs—that will reenergize or even re-create your operations—your way of seeing things, your way of thinking about things, and your ways of acting.

To encourage you and nudge you along in your change process, I am going to suggest a final battery of comments and exercises. These will sum up and help you implement, in synergistic fashion, the major techniques (or approaches) that make up the inner game.

USE ATTENTION AS A PRACTICAL TOOL

If awareness is the most fundamental tool in your kit, attention is the most practical. Attention is involved in all change worthy of the label "progress."

Attention is even involved in awareness. In order to be (more) aware, you must focus your attention on awareness. Focusing attention (the flashlight beam, remember?) is what allows you to become aware of your awareness.

Of the dozens available, jot down three to five ways to apply focus, or attention, to aspects of your business operation.

_____

_____

_____

_____

_____

Attention and awareness go together so naturally, in fact, it sometimes is difficult to mention one without talking about the other.

Besides being linked to awareness, however, attention can and should be synergized in all other areas: everything from focusing on mind-sets, to concentrating on feelings, to keeping an eye on habits, to achieving personal productivity.

As the needle of a compass points to true north, so attention will point you in the direction of your truest and best interests and concerns.

POST NOTES TO YOURSELF

It's amazing how a simple little thing like a note can reinforce a commitment or expand your awareness or focus your attention. You can post notes to yourself as reminders in your day planner, above or near your desk, as pop-up items on your computer screen, or on a message board.

Don't overwhelm yourself with too many notes on too many different subjects all at once. Concentrate, rather, on two or three things at a time. Everything you are working on, from organization to sales or marketing to people issues, is fair game. In your notes, try asking yourself these questions:

- Are you sitting up straight and smiling as you answer the phone? Remember, posture and facial expression communicates through the voice.
- What are you feeling right now about your efforts to end the clutter on your desk?
- How far have you come in changing that mind-set about holding back on cold calling?
- Do you think you are really listening to your staff today?
- Where are you *right now* in your commitment to yourself to cut back on junk food and give your body some real nutrients to run on?

If you are working on changing a particular mind-set, list the new mind-set you want to incorporate. If you are working on heightening awareness of your feelings, ask, "What are you feeling now about . . . ?" If you are hoping to motivate yourself or your people more strongly, address that issue. If you are working on improving your personal productivity (time management), suggest useful techniques to yourself (i.e., "Group your phone calls, don't scatter them." "Determine your best writing time for reports and letters and reserve that time for that purpose.").

Write a few notes to yourself right now—notes that, if you posted them and looked at them several times a day, would help usher in desirable change in mind-sets, habits, or systems.

Note 1: _____

_____

_____

Note 2: _____

_____

_____

Note 3: _____

_____

_____

TREAT YOURSELF TO GOOD FEELINGS

Why wait for success in business before you feel happy—or satisfied? It's better to be joyous all along the road to success. Be enthusiastic about your progress, large and small. Be confident about the results you are producing. Be satisfied with your life.

Does that sound difficult? You have the power to generate the feelings you would like to enjoy. Generating positive feelings is a learnable skill. Start with awareness, then focus your attention, add the processes for changing mind-sets from Step 3, and use your feelings discussed in Step 4.

One of the most important feelings a human being can generate is the feeling of thankfulness. Be grateful for all the results, all the little successes, you have had already. Create synergy: use being thankful for past progress to produce positive results today!

List things for which you can be thankful:
_____
_____
_____
_____
_____

Just writing out your list will put you in a more positive frame of mind. Doesn't it feel good?

ADD FEELINGS TO AFFIRMATIONS AND VISUALIZATIONS

Combine feelings synergistically with affirmations and visualizations; enjoy your triple-whammy power to achieve your goals. Let's say your goal is to acquire and renovate an old building with charm, have a space for your own venture, and rent out other spaces to other entrepreneurs.

First, call up the most intense feeling of satisfaction you could muster as you visualize your dream building already restored and filled with happy entrepreneurial tenants, and you operating your own business in their midst. Then write an affirmation to help evoke strong feelings of satisfaction and the vision of the completed building.

Post that affirmation where you will see it every day!

Such an affirmation might say, "Ah, how glorious it feels to have renovated a building of great character and charm, have it all rented out, and be able to work there myself!"

Are you catching on to how this all works?

Be sure to include feeling thankful that you have the dream, and grateful for any and all steps that help you make it come true.

BUILD MORE DESIRE—EVERYWHERE

Whenever possible, evoke the original fire that you used to launch your business. Stoke desire in all areas of your life. Build desire in your search for heightened self-awareness, in your efforts to sharpen your focus, in observing your self-talk, and in changing (for the better!) your mental models and your habits. Bring desire to the experiencing and expressing of your feelings.

Continue right on through your personal productivity, your fine-tuning (or outright overhauling) of the systems in your business. Bring desire to restyling your environment. And, finally, bring desire to your efforts to combine techniques in synergistic fashion.

Desire should be with you in everything you do.

APPLY INNER GAME TECHNIQUES ANYWHERE

Address any area of your business you please: any activity, any relationship, any system, any problem, any opportunity, any goal, anything at all. Then start going through the list of subjects we've covered, and apply the techniques detailed in this book, one by one or two or three, or more, synergistically. There are no limits. Further, all positive results will reinforce your conviction that the inner game techniques work! They will make a measurable difference. You can count on them. And they are your best allies in your quest for success, both as measured by sales volume or before tax income, or as a harmonious work atmosphere, or as shared values among staff and suppliers and customers.

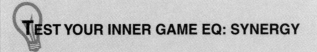

TEST YOUR INNER GAME EQ: SYNERGY

Rate yourself from 1 (weak) to 5 (strong) on how much each statement reflects your current state. Go with the first answer that comes to mind as you read each statement. Circle the number that best represents your capacity in each quiz item.

1. I am aware of synergy.   1 2 3 4 5
2. I understand how synergy can
   empower my business.   1 2 3 4 5
3. I see how synergy has worked
   in the past.   1 2 3 4 5
4. I notice synergy in action.   1 2 3 4 5
5. I am actively capitilizing on synergy.   1 2 3 4 5

Synergy total _____

Evaluating Your Inner Game EQ

Add up the totals for the quizzes at the end of each step. This will give you your grand total for all quizzes combined. The totals and grand total can be evaluated as follows:

TOTALS		GRAND TOTAL	
20–25	Excellent	200–250	You are a master of the Inner Game.
15–19	Great	150–199	You are playing the Inner Game very well but still have points to master.
10–14	Good	100–149	You are doing better than average.
5–9	Weak	50–99	You are at or below average (redo all exercises).
1–4	Very poor	1–49	Reread the book—twice!

Epilogue

Practice, Practice, Practice!

What do these people have in common—olympic athletes, best-selling novelists, and all people who become very good at what they do? They all know that the secret to mastering a challenge or reaching a goal is practice. It is the same for the techniques in this book. If they remain enshrined as words printed on paper, they will do you no good. *You* are the one who must transfer them into your consciousness and into your actions.

Thus, if you think something sounds like it should work, and you try it three or four times and you're not happy with the results, try again.

This book is not to be read through once and then put on a shelf to gather dust. Reread it often, as a whole or the section you need. Redo the exercises. Talk over all the steps with a reading partner or a business coach. Two heads are definitely better than one when it comes to training for the Inner Game (and three are better still!).

Godspeed on your journey. May success and prosperity be your companions on the road.

uggested Reading

BUSINESS DEVELOPMENT

The Fifth Discipline, by Peter Senge (Doubleday, 1990).
Making It on Your Own, by Paul and Sarah Edwards (Tarcher/Putnam, 1991).
Corporate Tides, by Robert Fritz (Berrett-Koehler, 1996).
The E-Myth Revisited, by Michael Gerber (HarperCollins, 1995).
Small Business Management Guide, by Jim Schell (Henry Holt, 1994).
How to Make 1,000 Mistakes in Business and Still Succeed, by Harold Wright (The Wright Track, 1990).
How to Get Clients, by Jeff Slutsky (Warner Books, 1992).
Growing a Business, by Paul Hawken (Simon & Schuster, 1987).

MANAGEMENT

Heart at Work, by Jack Canfield and Jacqueline Miller (McGraw-Hill, 1996).
The One-Minute Manger, by Kenneth Blanchard and Spencer Johnson (William Morrow, 1981).
Supra-Conscious Leadership, by James N. Farr, Ph.D. (Research Triangle Publishing, 1998).

Enlightened Leadership, by Ed Oakley and Doug Krug (Simon & Schuster, 1991).

The Art of Leadership, by Max DePree (Dell Publishing, 1989).

Zapp! The Lighting Power of Empowerment—How to Improve Quality, Productivity and Employee Satisfaction, by William C. Byham, Ph.D. (Ballantine, 1988).

Managing from the Heart, by Hyler Bracey, Jack Rosenblum, Aubrey Sanford, and Roy Trueblood (Dell Publishing, 1990).

INTERPERSONAL SKILLS

Everything You Need to Talk Your Way to Success, by Burton Kaplan (Prentice-Hall, 1995).

Why Didn't You Say That in the First Place—How to Be Understood at Work, by Richard Heyman (Jossey-Bass, 1994).

Communicate with Confidence, by Diana Booher (McGraw-Hill, 1994).

Introduction to Non-Violent Communication, by Marshall Rosenberg, audio (Center for Non-Violent Communication).

The Eight Essential Steps to Conflict Resolution, by Dudley Weeks (Putnam, 1993).

Hit the Ground Running, by Cynthia Kreuger (Brighton Publications, 1995).

Sell Your Way to the Top, by Zig Zigler, audio (Nightingale-Conant, 1986).

The Greatest Salesman in the World, by Og Mandino (Bantam Books, 1968).

How to Win Friends and Influence People, by Dale Carnegie (Simon & Schuster, 1936).

MIND POWER

Flow: The Psychology of Optimal Experience, by Mihaly Csikszentmihalyi (Harper & Row, 1990).
Dare to Win, by Mark Victor Hanson and Jack Canfield (Berkley Books, 1994).
Visualizing Is Realizing—What You See Is What You Get, by Mark Victor Hanson, audio (Mark Victor Hanson & Associates).
Unlimited Power, by Anthony Robbins, book/audio (Ballantine/Nightingale-Conant, 1986).
Your Secret Wealth—Hidden Assets and Opportunities That Can Change Your Life, by Jay Abraham, audio (Nightingale-Conant, 1994).
The Power of Your Supermind, by Vernon Howard (Prentice-Hall, 1975).
A Rich Man's Secret, by Ken Roberts (Llewellyn Publications, 1995).
The Seven Spiritual Laws of Success, by Deepak Chopra (Amber-Allen Publishing, 1994).
Imaging, by Norman Vincent Peale (Fleming H. Revell Company, 1982).
Release Your Brakes, by James W. Newman (Warner Books, 1977).
You Are What You Think, by Doug Hooper (Prentice-Hall, 1987).
You Can Have It All, by Arnold Patent (Celebration Publishing, 1991).
You'll See It When You Believe It, by Dr. Wayne W. Dyer (William Morrow, 1989).
The Psychology of Winning—Ten Qualities of a Total Winner, by Dr. Dennis Waitley, book/audio (Berkley Book/Nightingale-Conant, 1979).
Think and Grow Rich, by Napoleon Hill (Fawcett Crest, 1937).

FEELINGS

Emotional Intelligence, by Daniel Goleman (Bantam Books, 1995).
Emotional Intelligence at Work, by Hendrie Wessinger, Ph.D. (Jossey-Bass, 1998).
Achieving Emotional Literacy, by Claude Steiner, Ph.D. (Avon Books, 1997).
Facing the Fire, by John H. Lee (Bantam Books, 1993).
Feel the Fear and Do It Anyway, by Susan Jeffers (Harcourt Brace Jovanovich, 1987).

PERSONAL PRODUCTIVITY

The 7 Habits of Highly Effective People, by Stephen Covey (Fireside, 1989).
Time Tactics of Very Successful People, by B. Eugene Griessman (McGraw-Hill, 1994).
The Personal Efficiency Program, by Kerry Gleeson (John Wiley & Sons, 1994).
Self-Esteem and Peak Performance, by Jack Canfield, audio (CareerTrack, 1989).
Do It! Let's Get Off Our Buts, by Peter McWilliams (Prelude Press, 1991).
Getting Things Done, by Edwin Bliss (Maxwel Macmillian International, 1991).
Do It Now, by Dr. William J. Kraus (Prentice-Hall, 1979).

ENVIRONMENT

Health and Light, by John Ott (Devin-Adair, 1973).
The Psychology of Color and Design, by Deborah T. Sharpe (Nelson-Hall Company, 1974).
The Nontoxic Home & Office, by Debra Lynn Dadd (J.P. Tarcher, 1992).
Sick Building Syndrome, by Nicholas Tate (New Horizon Press, 1994).

MISCELLANEOUS

Life 101—Everything You Wish You Learned about Life in School But Didn't, by Peter McWilliams (Prelude Press, 1991).
Mastery, by George Leonard (Penguin Group, 1991).
Superlearning, by Shelia Ostrander and Lynn Schroeder (Dell Publishing, 1979).
Your Money or Your Life, by Hoe Dominguez and Vicki Robin (Penguin Books, 1992).
A Brief History of Everything, by Ken Wilber (Shambhala, 1996).

Index

A
Accomplishments, listing, 108–9
Action plans, 117–18
Affirmations, 48–49, 90, 185
Algebra, 138–39
"Americamania," 23
Anger, managing, 73–74
Aristotle, 74, 93
 Aristotelian logic, 44
Armstrong, Louis, 2
Attention, 15–31, 181–82. *See also* Awareness
 benefits of focused, 16
 communication skills and, 20–23
 conflict resolution and, 22–23
 flow and, 19–22
 keeping strong and focused, 23–26
 flow, 17–22
 key measure and, 30–31
 testing inner game EQ, 32
 work styles and, 26–30
Attitude(s). *See* Mind-sets
Aurelius, Marcus, 1, 39
Awareness, 1–13, 174–77. *See also* Attention
 flow and, 19–22
 increasing, 11–13
 linking with experience, 4–8
 as management skill, 2
 present level of, determining, 3–4
 prioritizing goals, 121–22
 resistance, 8–10
 of synergy, 174–77
 testing inner game EQ, 14

B
Bannister, Roger, 33
Behavior, effect of business systems on, 137
Beliefs. *See* Mind-sets
Blanchard, Ken, 158
Body language, 21
Body rhythms, 120
Business, evaluation of, 7–8
Business habits, 93–110
 associations with, 106
 awareness of, 95–96
 benefits of good, 100–102
 changing, 98–99
 coaches and, 106–7
 combining techniques, 109
 consequences for bad, 99
 cycles for altering behaviors, 96–97
 listing accomplishments, 108
 lying to yourself about, 102–3
 negative, 100–101
 positive, 101
 rewarding yourself for changing, 103–4

Business habits, *continued*
  testing inner game EQ, 110
  tracking results, 104
  visualizing end result of, 105
Business-building, fear of, 5
Business experience, 4–8
Business plan, 172–73
Business strategy, mind-sets and, 41–42
Business systems, 135–54
  dynamic complexity in, 138–41
  dynamic process of, 141–42
  feedback in, 142–48
    balancing, 147–48
    delay, 144–45
    reinforcing, 145–47
  grouping, 136
  importance of, 137–38
  interrelatedness of, 136–37
  leverage in, 151–53
  systems thinking, 148–51
  testing your inner game EQ, 154

C
Calculus, 139
Capital, 10
Carnegie, Andrew, 169
Change, 171–72
  productive, 180–81
Charts, 31, 107
Chesterton, G. K., 12
Churchill, Winston, 155
Coaches, 90, 106–7
Colors, psychology of, 164–65
Commoner, Barry, 135
Communication skills, 20–23, 182
  conflict resolution and, 22–23, 59–60
Community college small-business centers, 5

"Compassionate Communication," 59–60
Competence, 96–97
Concentration, 15. *See also* Attention
  heightening, 24–25
Conflict resolution, 22–23, 59–61
Consultants, fee-based small business, 5
Covey, Stephen, 34, 58, 117
Criticism, fear of, 5
Cross-training, 171–72
Csikszentmihalyi, Mihaly, 17–18
Cycles, performance and, 26–27

D
Deadlines, 124
Delegation, 131–33
Demming, W. Edwards, 104
Denial, 2, 5–6
  mind-sets and, 47
Desire, to accomplish, 79–91
  building mind-set for, 89, 185–86
  enthusiasm, excitement and, 83
  feelings triggered by, 83–84
  memories of, 84–85
  origin of, 80–82
  positive feelings and, 89–91
  raising level of, 82
  sales and, 86–87
  self-discipline and, 87–88
  self-motivation, 86
  testing inner game EQ, 92
  values and, 85
Detail complexity, 138
Diet, 25
Discipline, 87–88
Distraction(s), 112, 128–30
  tolerance, 30

INDEX 199

Dryden, John, 93
Dynamic complexity, 138–41

E
Ecology, 135
Efficiency, 135
Emotional Intelligence, 56
Emotional intelligence,
    improving, 61–65
  awareness of feelings, 63–64
  intensity of feelings,
    measuring, 64–65
Emotional Intelligence at Work,
    86
Emotions. *See* Feelings
Empathy, 76–77
Employees, feelings and,
    57–61
  conflict resolution, 59–61
  productivity, 58–59, 61
Energy
  lack of, 24
  levels, 156–57. *See also* Work
    environment, energizing
Enthusiasm. *See* Desire, to
    accomplish
Environment. *See* Work
    environment, energizing
Euripides, 39
Exercise, 25
Experience
  associating perceptions and,
    37
  linking with awareness, 4–8
Exponential change, 171–72

F
Facilitator, 131
*Facing the Fire: Experiencing
  and Expressing Anger
  Appropriately*, 73
Fears, 5
  managing, 74–75

  procrastination and, 126–28
  of success, 150
Feedback, 142–48
  balancing, 147–48
  delay, 144–45
  reinforcing, 145–47
  synergy and, 173
Feelings, 54–78
  adding to affirmations and
    visualizations, 185
  awareness of others', 76–77
  emotional intelligence and,
    61–65
    awareness of feelings,
      63–64
    feedback, 64
    measuring intensity of
      feelings, 64–65
  employees and, 57–61
    conflict resolution, 59–61
    productivity, 58–59, 61
  expressing, 65–68
  importance of, to business,
    56–57
  as language of relationships,
    55–56
  managing, 71–75
    anger, 73–74
    fear, 74–75
    redirecting feelings, 72–73
  negativism, 84, 89
  positive, creating, 89, 184
  remembered, 75
  testing inner game EQ, 78
  vocabulary of, 69–71
Feng Shui, 162–63
Fifth Dimension, The, 136
Financial considerations,
    mind-sets and, 150
Flow, 17–22
  "Americamania" and, 23
  applications for
    entrepreneurs, 18–19

Flow, *continued*
 linking awareness and
  attention with, 19–22
*Flow: The Psychology of
 Optimal Experience,* 17–18
Fluorescent lighting, 165–66
Focus, 122–23. *See also*
 Attention
Ford, Henry, 34
Frankl, Viktor, 40
Fun, on the job, 91
Furniture arrangement, 162–63

G
Gantt chart, 31
Goals, 113–18
 action plans, 117–18
 focus and, 122–23
 implicit, 148, 150–51
 levels of, 113–14
 mind-sets that inhibit
  achievement of, 36
 prioritizing, 120–25
 revising, as business
  develops, 114
 synergy and, 176
 target dates, 117
 to-do lists and, 118–19
Goleman, Daniel, 56
Graphs, 31,107
Griessman, Eugene, 119

H–I
Habits
 business. *See* Business
  habits
 mental. *See* Mind-sets
Health problems, 24
Hidden agendas, 148, 150–51
Human systems, 136
Hurt, feeling of, 73
Incandescent lighting, 165–66

Incompetence, 96
Interruptions, 30, 128–30
 telephone, 129–30

J–K
Johnson, Spencer, 158
Jung, Carl, 54
Kakuzo, Okakura, 135
Kentucky Fried Chicken, 172
Key measure, 30–31, 104, 107

L
Laziness, 5
Learning curves, 174–77
Lee, John, 73
Leverage, in business systems,
 151–53
Lighting, effects of, 165–66
Lincoln, Abraham, 111
Linear change, 171
Listening skills, 20–21
 coaches and, 107

M
Management skills. *See*
 Awareness
Man's Search for Himself
 (May), 69
Man's Search for Meaning
 (Frankl), 40
Marden, Orison Swett, 94
May, Rollo, 69
Meditation, 11–12, 25
Meetings, 131–33
Mental exercise, 25
Mental models. *See* Mind-sets
Micromanaging, 133
Mind-sets, 33–53, 150, 173–79
 acquiring, 40–41
 being always "right," 43
 business strategy affected
  by, 41

changing, 45–50, 98
for entrepreneurs, 51
evaluating mental models, 44–45
modeling people with successful, 50–51
outdated, 39
perceptions and, 34–37
as reality filter, 37–40
testing inner game EQ, 53
that spur business, 38
synergy and, 178–79
"Model for Nonviolent Communication, A," 59
Money, expressions regarding, 34–35
Morale, 135

N–O

Negativism, 84
Newton, Sir Isaac, 4
Nicklaus, Jack, 49–50
Nicomachean Ethics, 93
Noise, 25–26
"Nonviolent Communication," 59
Numbers, tracking, 30–31
Nutrition, 25
One Minute Manager, The, 158
Operational systems, 136
Orderliness, in work environment, 159
Ott, John, 165–66

P–Q

Pace, 28
Passion. *See* Desire, to accomplish
Patience, 52
Peak hours, 26–27
People contact, 28–29
People Express airline, 2–3

Perceptions, mind-sets and, 34–37
Persistence, 51–52
Planners, 118
Plant life, 167
Practice, importance of, 189
Prejudice, 46–47. *See also* Mind-sets
Prioritizing, 24, 119
goals, 120–25
Procrastination, 126–28
Production, increased, 26
Productivity, 58–61, 111–34, 135, 186. *See also* Synergy
goals, 113–18
interruptions and, 128–30
meetings and, 131–33
prioritizing, 120–25
procrastination, curing, 126–28
target dates and, 117
testing inner game EQ, 134
to-do lists, 118–19
Project variety, 29–30
Quality, in work environment, 161–62
Questions, listening skills, and, 21

R

Reality, filtered by mind-sets, 37–40
Recreation, 90–91
Resources, 191–92
Responsibility, 150
Review organizations, 5
Rhythmic breathing, 25
Rich Man's Secret, A, 3
Risks, 2, 41
Robbins, Anthony, 106
Roberts, Ken, 3
Role models, 42, 50–51

Rosenberg, Marshall B., 59–60
Routines, 123–24

S
Sales calls, tracking, 31
Schedules, 123–24
SCORE, 5
Self-discipline, 87–88
Self-discovery, 179–80
Self-fulfilling prophecies, 34
Self-motivation. *See* Desire, to accomplish
Self-talk, 75, 89–90
  habits and, 102–3
  negative, eliminating, 89, 108
Senge, Peter, 136, 151
Service Corps of Retired Executives (SCORE), 5
Shakespeare, 79
Sheehan, George A., 25
"Sick buildings," 166–67
Small business centers, 5
Smith, Adam, 170
Smoke-free environments, 167
Spenser, Edmund, 33
Statistics, tracking, 30–31
Strategic actions, 151
Strategy (business), mind-sets and, 41–42
Strength
  of attention, 23
  awareness of, 10–11
Stress, 59
Synergy, 169–87
  affirmations, feelings, visualizations and, 185
  application of inner game techniques and, 172–74
  attention and, 181–82
  awareness of, 174–75
  building desire, 185–86
  exponential results with, 171–72
  goals and, 176
  learning curves, 174
  mind-sets and 178
  positivism, 184
  posting notes to yourself, 182–83
  productive change and, 180–81
  self-discovery and, 179–80
  testing inner game EQ, 187
Systems. *See* Business systems
Systems thinking, 148–51

T
Target dates, 117
Technical systems, 136
Telephone interruptions, 129–30
Thankfulness, 184
Time management, 24, 111
Time Tactics of Very Successful People, 119
To-do lists, 118–19
Tracking, statistics/numbers and, 30–31, 104

U–V
U.S. Chamber of Commerce, manager and employee survey by, 57–58
U.S. Labor Department, employee survey by, 57
Unawareness, 2
Unlimited Power, 106
Values, 85
Visual displays, 31, 104
Visualization, 49–50, 90, 105, 107, 185
Vocabulary, of feelings, 69–71

W-Y

Water, drinking, 25
Watt, Clement, 3
Wealth of Nations, The, 170
Weisinger, Heindre, 86
Work environment, energizing, 155–68
  colors, psychology of, 164–65
  furniture arrangement, 162–63
  lighting, effects of, 165–66
  measuring energy levels, 156–57
  mood creation, 157–59
  orderliness, 159
  plant life, 167
  purpose of workplace, considering, 160–61
  quality in environment, 161–62
  sick buildings, avoiding, 166–67
  testing inner game EQ, 168
Work styles, and attention, 26–30
  distraction tolerance, 30
  duration, 28
  pace, 28
  peak hours, 26–27, 120–21
  people contact, 28–29
  project variety, 29–30
"Yes" exercise, 90